THOMAS ANDERSON

ELEPHANT PATHS

COMBAT HISTORY OF
STURMGESCHÜTZ-ABTEILUNG 203

peko
PUBLISHING

© PeKo Publishing Kft.
Published by PeKo Publishing Kft.
8360 Keszthely, Bessenyei György utca 37., Hungary
Email: info@pekobooks.com
www.pekobooks.com

Author: Thomas Anderson
Editing: Derik Hammond

Photos:
Florian von Aufseß, Yves Beraud, Henry Hoppe, Péter Kocsis, Karlheinz Münch,
Peter Müller, Jason D. Mark, Wolfgang Schneider, Markus Zöllner,
Heinz Angelmaier, Sergei Netrebenko, Photo Archiv Sturmartillerie,
National Archives

Printed in Hungary
First published: 2022
ISBN 978-615-5583-75-9

TABLE OF CONTENT

GLOSSARY

Artillerie-Lehrregiment (ALR)	instructional regiment of the artillery
Generalstab des Heeres (GenStdH)	General Staff of the Army (Heerestruppen)
(-Ebene)	army troop (level)
Kriegstärkenachweisung (KStN)	organisational structure
Leichter gepanzerter Beobachtungs-Kraftwagen (le gep BeobKw, SdKfz 253)	light armoured observation vehicle
Leichter gepanzerter Munitions-Kraftwagen (le gep MunKw, SdKfz 252)	light armoured ammunition vehicle
mittlerer geländegängiger Personenkraftwagen (m Pkw, gl)	medium cross-country car
Panzergrenadier (PzGren)	armoured infantry
Panzerjäger (PzJg)	tank destroyer
Panzertruppe (PzTrp)	armoured forces
schwere Zugkraftwagen 18 t (s ZgKw 18 t, SdKfz 9)	heavy prime mover
Stab (Stb)	staff
Stabsbatterie (StbsBttr)	staff battery
Sturmgeschütz(e) (StuG)	assault gun(s)
Sturmartillerie (StuArt)	assault artillery
Sturmbatterie (StuBttr), or Sturmgeschütz-Batterie (StuGBttr)	assault gun battery
Sturmartillerie-Abteilung (StuArtAbt)	assault artillery battalion, former name of
Sturmgeschütz-Abteilung (StuGAbt)	assault gun battalion
Sturmartillerie-Brigade (StuGBrig)	assault artillery brigade
Sturmgeschütz Ersatz- und Ausbildungs-Abteilung (StuGErsAusbAbt)	assault gun training and replacement btl
Tiefladeranhänger	low-bed trailer
Waffenamt (WaA)	Ordnance Bureau
Zugführer	platoon leader

INTRODUCTION

Elephant Paths: the title of this book refers to the unit symbol of StuGAbt 203, later redesignated StuGBrig 203, a charging elephant. The unit displayed this coat of arms proudly on their Sturmgeschütze and other vehicles during the often hard fighting on the Eastern Front.

Basic considerations

Readers interested in the history of German military formations can choose between different sources. The book market offers a wide variety of publications, many of which are based on the personal recollections of veterans or on information already published in other books which has the potential to create its own problems. Internet-based publications then copy the information contained in these sources. However, the historian, and also the author, is obliged to refer to other sources. Utilizing the memories of surviving soldiers was only possible over a limited time frame which spanned the period from the end of the war to the 1990s by which time they had grown very old. Here, however, a fundamental problem arose. With the passage of time those personal recollections could be vague, exaggerated, or simply imprecise. False "facts" should however never be the basis of historical works.

The "official" unit histories published by veteran's associations are another source of information.

After the war many surviving German soldiers formed veterans' associations which often reflected the traditions of their old units. In case of the Sturmartillerie, the men of the former 45 assault gun battalions established an umbrella association, the "Gemeinschaft der Sturmartillerie" in Karlstadt, which at that time was in Western Germany.

The author was able to meet many veterans there, and attended some of their meetings.

Other sources are the national archives of former combatants. The Western Allies preyed on large stocks of German documents which were then mostly stored in the US. These documents were microfilmed and made accessible to the public. In the 1960s the originals were given back to Germany and they are now stored in the Bundesarchiv/ Militärarchiv in Freiburg. However, apart from a few exceptions, the history of smaller units, such as the battalion-sized Sturmgeschütz-Abteilungen, were not documented in this inventory. These countless files were stored in the large Heeresarchiv Potsdam, which was destroyed during a bomb attack in 1945.

The Geschützführer (commander) of a Sturmgeschütz (lang); next to him the muzzle brake of the 7.5 cm StuK 40 L/48. The Unteroffizier (non-commissioned officer) uses his double telescope to observe the battlefield.

The victorious Soviet Union also collected documents. By 1945 the remnants of the bombed and burned Heeresarchiv Potsdam had been searched and the archival documents, some in a very bad state, were transported to various locations. Some years ago

Russia decided to make these documents available to the public. After scanning the original documents, the digitized reproductions were uploaded to a website hosted by the Central Archive of the Ministry of Defence of the Russian Federation (CAMO).

Considered as a whole, these files contain an immense wealth of knowledge and are an essential foundation for any scientific research in this wide field.

Consequently the author felt it necessary to research the information held in the surviving files at the BAMA in Freiburg, the NARA in Alexandria and the CAMO in Podolsk.

The designation of the units changed repeatedly during their service lives. The author uses these designations according to their usage at the time. Furthermore the terms "unit", "Abteilung" (battalion) and "Brigade" are used in this publication.

Acknowledgements

The tables of organization were compiled through careful interpretation of those KStN (Kriegstärkenachweisungen – German tables of organization) still available today, and other German war reporting. Discrepancies in the documents are both possible and likely. All symbols shown in the tables were in use in wartime documents.

The author also wishes to express his appreciation to the following individuals who provided assistance, advice or photographs. Contacts with the Verband der Sturmartillerie (Association of Sturmartillerie Veterans) were invaluable; I was able to find wartime records, war diaries and, above all, many friends among the now elderly gentlemen who fought in these armoured vehicles.

The author received material and photos from many individuals and would like to express his sincere appreciation, in particular, to:

Florian von Aufseß
Yves Beraud
Henry Hoppe
Peter Kocsis
Karlheinz Münch
Peter Müller

Orientation in the vastness of the Eastern Front posed great problems for combat troops and supply units of all kinds. Signs were normal in all towns and traffic junctions.

Sturmartillerie – a new service of arms

Sturmgeschütze (assault guns) were designed as armoured support weapons to assist infantry attacks. The technical solution was straightforward and simple– an infantry support gun was mounted on an armoured motorized chassis. The concept shared many features with the earlier infantry tank, which had emerged during WW I, and which was still in the inventories of many nations. Sturmgeschütze had, however, no rotating turret, which saved weight but reduced their range of applications.

The new assault guns were to be organized in a new specialized service of arms, the Sturmartillerie (assault artillery). A document dated 16 June 1936 of the GenStdH explains:

1. Essentially we agree on the ideas and the technical development of the Sturmgeschütz and its tactical commitment.

2. It however seems necessary to emphasize the following distinctive differences to the divisional artillery, and to give the Waffenamt simple and clear requirements for the development process of the Sturmgeschütz.
   a.) The Sturmartillerie has the task to annihilate enemy machine guns with targeted direct fire. This task will be executed in the range of the infantry over distances up to 4 km. Thus Sturmgeschütze are weapons of the infantry.
   They won´t be available to solve artillery missions. For this reason there is no need for the ability to fire using indirect means of observation at ranges up to 7 km.
   b.) Simultaneously the Sturmartillerie must be able to fully replace the divisional Panzerjäger (tank destroyer) elements, which are currently under development.

3. There are no reservations against the planned troop trial…

The General Staff of the Army emphasized a clear division of responsibilities. According to the lines above, Sturmgeschütze were intended to be a subordinate support arm of the infantry. While the tank (in the sense of the German Panzertruppe) would break through the enemy lines, the Sturmgeschütz would push forward the infantry´s assault.

According to these documents of 1936, Sturmgeschütze would not be concentrated in great numbers, but only platoonwise. Each infantry division was to have one StuGAbt with three batteries each of which was equipped with six Sturmgeschütze.

The proposed troop trial was conducted by mounting wooden dummies on available tank chassis. Following the success of these tests, the production of Sturmgeschütze was ordered by 1938.

The inability of the German arms industry to fulfill all armaments projects led to a prioritization of the Panzertruppe which meant that production of Sturmgeschütze only began after significant delays and at a slow pace.

Consequently, during the mobilization in 1939, it was not possible to allocate StuGAbt to the infantry divisions.

The original deployment principles set up by 1936 would remain valid only in parts. By April 1940 the instructional pamphlet "Richtlinien für den Einsatz der Sturmartillerie" (principles for the commitment of the assault artillery) was published, which weakened many of these rules. The new manual rigorously reduced the combat against enemy tanks to self-defence, but allowed deployment for limited artillery missions.

Beginning in January 1940, a first 0-series of 30 assault guns was produced. In order to allot Sturmgeschütze to as many units as possible, several (first five, then six) batteries of six assault guns each were established. In principle these independent units were organized on army troop level, a blueprint for the later deployment of the battalion-size StuGAbt.

The first commitments during the invasion of France were positive and, following increased Sturmgeschütz production, the first Sturmgeschütz-Abteilungen were established. Apart from a few exceptions, all future StuG units would remain at army troop level but could be temporarily subordinated to infantry (and tank) divisions on a case-by-case basis. This applied only to StuG units of the artillery. From 1943 assault guns were also issued to Panzer, Panzergrenadier and Panzerjäger units.

Sturmgeschütze greifen an (assault guns attack)! This unknown unit simulates a massive advance in wedge formation. The commander and gunner watch from their open hatches, steel helmets on.

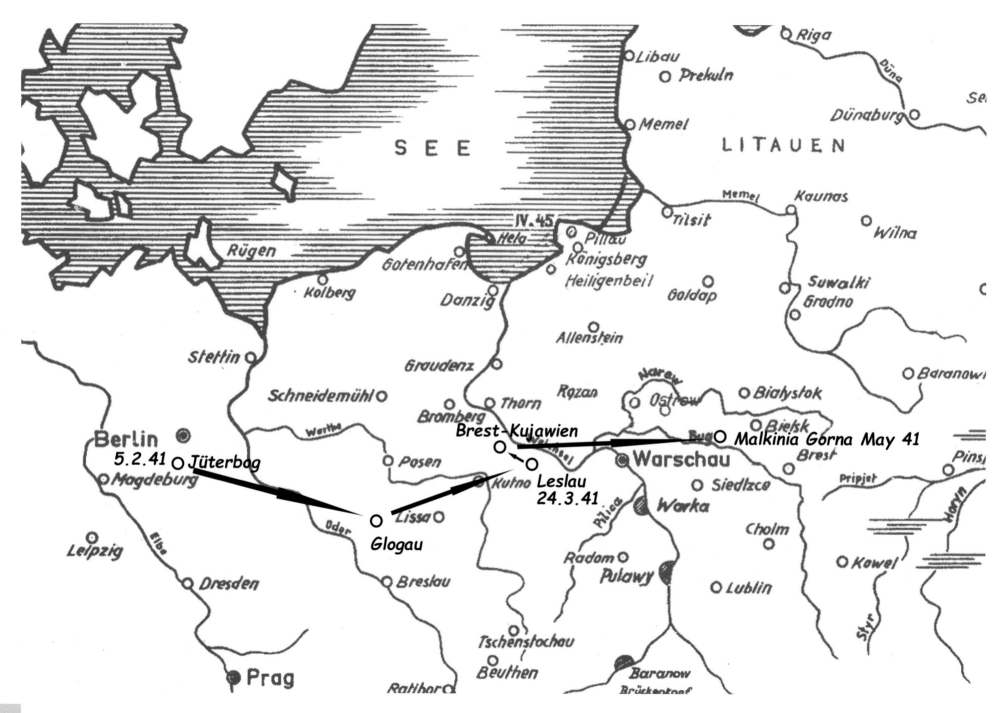

SEE

LITAUEN

Riga
Libau
Prekuln
Düna
Dünaburg
Memel
Se

IV.45
Helg
Pillau
Memel
Kaunas
Tilsit
Wilna

Rügen
Gotenhafen
Königsberg
Heiligenbeil
Suwalki
Goldap
Grodno

Kolberg
Danzig

Allenstein

Stettin
Graudenz
Rozan
Narew
Ostrow
Bialystok
Baranowi

Schneidemühl
Thorn
Bielsk

Werthe
Bromberg
Brest-Kujawien
Bug
Malkinia Gorna May 41
Brest

Berlin
5.2.41 Jüterbog
Posen
Kutno
Leslau
24.3.41
Warschau
Pinsk
Pripjet

Magdeburg
Oder
Lissa
Glogau
Warka
Siedlzce
Haryn

Leipzig
Elbe
Breslau
Pilica
Cholm

Dresden
Radom
Pulawy
Kowel
Lublin
Styr

Prag
Tschenstochau
Beuthen
Baranow
Brückenkopf
Ratibor

ESTABLISHMENT
OF STURMARTILLERIE-ABTEILUNG 203

CHAPTER 1

The original doctrine saw the assignment of StuG battalions to every infantry division. Due to the inadequate production situation in the Reich these ideas had to be dropped rather soon. Instead, the support units would be provided as Heerestruppen (army troops), independent units at army or corps level.

When, by early 1940, the first assault guns were available in limited numbers it was decided to use them to create battery-sized units (Sturmbatterie 640, 659, 660, 665, 666 and 667). A possible reason for this was the wish to gain first-hand experience with a greater number of smaller detachments subordinated under various infantry or tank divisions.

Beginning in August 1940, after the invasion of France, the first two battalion-sized assault gun units (StuArtAbt 184 and 185) were established. In September StuArtAbt 202 followed, by October 190 and 191, by November 192 and 197, and by December 209.

The establishment of the later Elephant Brigade started by 5 February 1941 under the designation Sturmartillerie-Abteilung 203 (StuArtAbt). Two days later a decision was made to undertake a general redesignation of these units. The six independent Sturmbatterien were now called Sturmgeschütz-Batterien (StuGBttr) and the StuArtAbt was changed to Sturmgeschütz-Abteilung (StuGAbt). The reason for this decision is unknown.

Like all other Sturmgeschütz units, Sturmgeschütz-Abteilung 203 was independent as part of army troops.

In common with its predecessor units, StuGAbt 203 was established in the Artillerie-Lehrregiment (ALR) in Jüterbog, home of the artillery school.

The training and replacement unit was the VI./ALR. Two months later a newly formed and more efficient training unit, StuG Ers und AusbAbt 200 in Schweinfurt, took over. During the war four such units were made available to the assault artillery with the intention to provide new personnel for further establishments and to replace the losses of the front units.

StuG Ers und AusbAbt 200 (Schweinfurt)
StuG Ers und AusbAbt 300 (Neiße)
StuG Ers und AusbAbt 400 (Haldensleben)
StuG Ers und AusbAbt 500 (Posen)

Organizational issues

German units were organized according to standardized organizational structures. The *Kriegsstärkenachweisung* (KStN, or table of organization) involved the actual furnishing with vehicles, weapons and men. The far more comprehensive *Kriegsausrüstungsnachweisung* (KAN) described all basic materiel allowances to a unit. The latter included almost any item of materiel from typewriter to torches. These tables of organization were frequently modified, modernized or adapted to new requirements.

Although the KStN would schedule the exact type of vehicle, the desperate supply situation would often not allow delivery of the intended materiel. Many units had to be content with similar materiel of lower adequacy or quality.

During combat, German units kept and updated lists of their materiel situation, giving higher levels of command exact information on the number and state of their combat vehicles. However, it was quite normal that these strength reports were faked by units keeping surplus vehicles secret or withholding captured enemy materiel to improve their own situation.

According to the KStN valid in early 1941, StuGAbt 203 had the following organization:

KStN 416 Stab StuGBttr dated 4 July 1940	- staff
KStN 444 StbsBttr dated 4 July 1940	- staff battery
KStN 446 StuGBttr dated 8 July 1940	- combat battery, three per Abteilung

This composition allowed, within certain limits, the independent commitment of the unit. Besides assault guns and their armoured support vehicles, the unit had a complete workshop platoon with recovery services. When single combat batteries were attached to an infantry division, a Bergezug and an InstZug (recovery and workshop section) could be also assigned.

Further support weapons such as infantry, conventional artillery and anti-aircraft artillery were not provided. Having in mind the original purpose of the assault artillery, this was not necessary.

After the orders for the establishment of Sturmartillerie-Abteilung 203 were given, a Vorkommando (advance party) prepared the situation. Apart from the staff personnel the unit consisted mainly of volunteers. Accordingly, the men, NCOs and officers were highly motivated.

Leading personal:

Battalion Commander	- Major Krokisius
Commander staff battery	- OLt Behnke
Commander 1. Bttr	- OLt Freiherr von Gleichenstein
Commander 2. Bttr	- OLt Dostler
Commander 3. Bttr	- OLt Wirth

The Abteilung moved into accommodation in Dorf Zinna on the Jüterbog training area. Formerly a small village, whose population was ousted by the founding of the manoeuver site at the end of the 19th century, barracks and vehicle halls were erected among its old houses.

Jüterbog - home of the Sturmartillerie (assault artillery). This postcard shows the small town to the south of Berlin. The Artillerieschule des Heeres (army artillery school) was stationed here, and in 1937 the assault artillery school was also to be launched here. From 1939 onwards, the first assault gun units began to be formed.

Dorf Zinna (the village Zinna) was one of the settlements that had to make way for the artillery firing range during the expansion of the military training area. The buildings were not inhabited; they were used for the training of the units practising here. After the war, the village was revived by refugees.

Since Hitler had already decided on war against Russia, orders were given to proceed with the establishment of Sturmartillerie-Abteilung 203 as quickly as possible. However, at that time only members of the general staff were informed. Veterans remembered that after the defeat of France no one, neither the public nor the lower ranks of the military, expected the war to go on. Indeed even parts of the ordnance office were not involved in the Führer's planning, since documents preparing the shape of the "future peacetime army" were published by end of 1940.

During February, Sturmartillerie-Abteilung 203 received its equipment.

Stab and Stabsbatterie (staff and staff battery)

The staff and staff battery consisted mainly of standard cross-country cars and 3 t trucks. The combat train had six 3 t trucks and an antiaircraft vehicle armed with twin MG 34 machine guns. The workshop section provided mechanical services for the complete Abteilung. Its recovery section was provided with three schwere Bergezüge (heavy recovery teams), consisting of schwere Zugkraftwagen 18 t (SdKfz 9) and Tieflader-anhänger for PzKpfw 22 t (SdAnh 116). When the combat batteries were delegated to separate infantry units these services, especially the recovery teams, were normally split up.

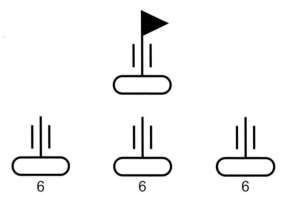

Sturmgeschütz-Abteilung
(18 StuG) basic organization as of July 1940

6   6   6

On the Zinna village square, roll calls of all assault gun units deployed in Jüterbog took place, here the formation training on the firing range started.

Gefechtsbatterien (combat batteries)

18 Sturmgeschütze were ready to be picked up at the manufacturer Alkett in Berlin-Borsigwalde. This was a great problem, since apart from a few senior NCOs and officers the unit had virtually no trained personnel. The Abteilung arranged a transfer team which was sent to Berlin. Here company employees assumed the task of instructing the soldiers. During their few days in Berlin the crews of 203 got accustomed to their new equipment.

The light armoured observation and ammunition vehicles, le gep Beobkw (SdKfz 253) observation vehicles and le gep MunKw (SdKfz 252) ammunition vehicles, waited in the Heereszeugamt (ordnance depots) in Magdeburg and Braunschweig. Photos from the phase of establishment prove that 203 had received the intended provision with nine le gep BeobKw and nine, or possibly 18, le gep MunKw. If a reduced number of MunKw was assigned, the missing vehicles were normally substituted by le ZgKw 1t (SdKfz 10). However, there is no photographic evidence that 203 received these vehicles.

Softskinned vehicles were delivered directly to Jüterbog where the men accepted them. The organizational structure scheduled mittlere geländegängige Personenkraftwagen (m Pkw gl, medium cross-country cars), Kfz 12 and Kfz 15 (radio cars). Apparently this was not possible at that time so the unit was provided with commercial vehicles instead. These 1930 vintage light, cross-country cars had only 4x2 drive and were a poor alternative.

The three m ZgKw 3 t (SdKfz 11) normally allotted to transport assault gun replacement crews can also not be verified by photos.

In the following weeks concentrated and condensed training took place in Jüterbog.

Due to the severe fuel shortage the new drivers were given only little opportunity to learn how to operate the tracked and half-tracked vehicles. Together with the workshop section they examined engines and transmissions and all maintenance was done together.

The standard 3 t trucks were delivered with open cargo bodies. Some were partly customized by the unit. For example, field kitchens were mounted on top of trucks and the workshop trucks were provided with wooden bodies.

When StuArt Abt 203 was first equipped at the beginning of 1941, only StuG Ausf B were delivered. This vehicle already shows the wider 40 cm tracks. Apart from the Balkenkreuz (German crosses) no markings have been applied yet.

The training of the new unit took place at the Artillerie-Lehr-Regiment (ALR, Artillery Training Regiment). Initially, only Ausf A vehicles were assigned to this training unit. Like the PzKpfw III Ausf E and F, the Maybach SRG 32 preselector gearbox was fitted, which allowed top speeds of up to 70 km/h - at the expense of the vulnerable chassis components.

The Sturmgeschütz, the weapon of the assault artillery. This Ausf C with the chassis number 90578 already shows the later suspension with the new 40 cm track and the correspondingly wider running wheels. The brand new vehicle was produced in May 1941 and did not go to the StuArt Abt 203.

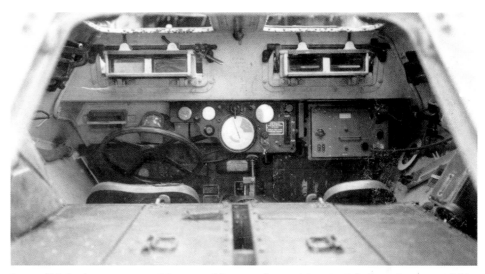

The basic tactical concept of the Sturmartillerie assigned a le gep BeobKw (SdKfz 253) to each battery and platoon commander as a radio and command vehicle. The lightly armoured half-track vehicles were equipped with long-range radios. StuArt Abt 203 also initially received nine or twelve of these vehicles.

In parallel, leichte gepanzerte Munitionsfahrzeuge (le gep MunKw, SdKfz 252) were available. These light armoured ammunition vehicles could carry 64 7.5cm grenades in the rear part of the interior. In a small trailer (SdAnh 32) another 64 grenades could be stowed. The initial equipment provided for 18 of these vehicles per Sturmartillerie-Abteilung (assault artillery battalion), a goal that was barely reached.

Three recovery trains, each with a s. ZgKw 18 t (SdKfz 9) and a low-bed trailer 22 t (SdAnh 116), were assigned to the Sturmgeschütz-Abteilungen. The unit was renamed Sturmgeschütz-Abteilung 203 (StuGAbt) in February 1941.

StuArt Abt 203 began training using the materiel pool of the Artillerie-Lehr-Regiment (ALR). This assault gun is an Ausf A2, which was built on PzKpfw III Ausf G hulls. To bring the hull front to the required thickness of 50 mm, 20 mm additional plates were bolted on.

Platoon training! Men of StuArt Abt 203 train on two Sturmgeschütz Ausf A2 of the ALR in winter 1940/41. In the background on the left is the platoon leader's SdKfz 253; the supply of ammunition is apparently ensured by a le. ZgKw 1 t (SdKfz 10).

At the Artillery Training Regiment standard situations were drilled. Here an Ausf A2 assault gun has driven backwards into cover, the additional armour is clearly visible. An ammunition tractor has driven up with ammunition; the SdAnh 32 trailer with 64 7.5 cm shells is clearly visible.

Wachtmeister (Sergeant) Jörner of 1./StuArt Abt 203 in January 1941 in front of a StuG Ausf B of the Artillery Training Regiment. The training unit used a bombarde in an oak wreath as its symbol, here stencilled on the superstructure front.

The training in Jüterbog also included the recovery of stuck assault guns. In this training situation, the vehicle on the right broke down on a wet meadow. Actually, it was forbidden to use tanks or assault guns for towing for reasons of materiel conservation. When the situation required it, prohibitions of this kind were gladly ignored.

This was also a standard situation. To repair a damaged chain, the open ends had to be closed with a chain clamp. Then the track pin was hammered in. Every tank was equipped with this track tool.

The initial equipment of StuArt Abt 203 was available at the beginning of 1941. At first, a simple chalk marking was applied at the Heeres-Zeugamt Magdeburg. The driving lights of the assault guns up to Ausf F were protected against damage by sheet metal covers.

Parts of the repair and recovery platoon of StuArt Abt 203. The unit is largely equipped with partially militarized, rear-wheel drive vehicles of dubious off-road capability. The platoon leader drives an Opel Kadett, a civilian vehicle. The heavy tractors are missing.

These men of Abt 203 still wore the black safety rubber core berets during training in Jüterbog. The protective headgear was never to be introduced comprehensively for unknown reasons.

The ALR's infirmary was located in the village of Zinna in March 1941. In action, the Abteilung was dependent on the services of larger units. In confusing situations near the front this could lead to dangerous delays.

The Abteilungsarzt (battalion doctor) of StuArt Abt 203, Dr. Gärtner. The officer wears the field-grey uniform of the assault artillery, the cut of which corresponded to that of the Sonderbekleidung der Panzertruppen (special clothing of the armoured troops).

After being assigned with its own assault guns in spring 1941, training of the Abteilung continued. In some cases, normal field uniforms were worn, which were absolutely unsuitable in very cold weather. Even before Moscow, only a few months later, the supply situation had not improved.

Ausf B assault guns in the technical section of the Artillery Training Regiment in Jüterbog. The vehicles were assigned to the newly formed units here. After the formation was completed, the Abteilungen were transported by rail to the theatre of operations.

The light armoured ammunition vehicles (SdKfz 252) were developed exclusively to supply the assault guns on the battlefield. The 14.5mm armour protected only against fire from 7.92mm SmK ammunition (armour-piercing infantry ammunition).

In spring 1941, trucks were also delivered to the Abteilung. Under the direction of Lt Kaatz, these were adapted to the requirements. The platform on the right was equipped with a self-built installation for the workshop.

Lt Kaatz was the motor transport officer of StuGAbt 203. The engineer headed the maintenance platoon.

Signalmen of Abteilung 203 train on the portable d2 (TornFuG d2) radio. The radio was made up of two parts: the transmitter/receiver in the front and the equipment pack with the battery in the back. When the unit was deployed to the east, it was replaced by the single-load TornFuG h.

The two-piece Sonderbekleidung für Sturmgeschütz-Besatzungen (special clothing for assault gun crews) was designed to be very simple. There were no pockets on the outside so as not to be a hindrance in the confines of the armoured vehicle.

TRANSPORT TO THE EAST

CHAPTER 2

By around 20 March 1941 the Abteilung was ready for the journey. All vehicles were loaded onto several trains. The transport travelled via Glogau (Głogów) to Leslau (Włocławek), where the unit was unloaded by 24 March.

The complete Abteilung moved into accommodation in and around the town with parts of it having to live in tents. Major Krokisius and his staff were quartered in the estate of the chief of the local sugar refinery.

Despite the fact that Poland was occupied, relations with the local population were apparently good. On one occasion Olt Peetz took a Sturmgeschütz and picked up the sugar refinery's plant manager for a tour through the still snowy landscape.

The unit proceeded with wireless and weapons training. At that time nobody could foresee that another major military conflict was at hand. However, the higher staffs were instructed to plan attack operations over the border. Documents found in different war diaries trivialized these measures as follows:

This picture of members of StuGAbt 203 was taken in Leslau, a few days after the eastward march in February 1943. Only two men of the gun squadron wear the special clothing, the others normal field uniforms. Perhaps they are members of the supply squadron.

> *VII. AK Korps HQ*
> *24 April 1941*
> *Korps order for the reconnaissance for combat or VII. Korps*
> *A.) Preliminary remarks regarding secrecy*
> *All deployments for an attack crossing the Reich's borders heading east are only a precautionary measure to be prepared for a sudden change of the Soviet Union's attitude to the German Reich… The following orders must be kept top secret. Only the divisional commanders and their general staff officers may be informed…*

In March 1941 orders were given to transfer StuGAbt 203 to the east. The destination was Brest-Kujawien (now Brześć Kujawski), a town some 180 km north-west of Warsaw. At that time only higher command levels were inducted in the plans of the German leadership. All preparations for the coming invasion such as troop deferrals and concentration in the eastern provinces were disguised as exercises or precautionary measure for a possible change of the Soviet Union's attitude against the Reich.

By May 1941 StuGAbt 203 had been transferred to Małkinia Górna, a village east of Warsaw and 100 km west of the Polish-Soviet border. Here, in the endless Polish forests, the `Waldlager´ (forest camp) was established. The nearby Bug River formed the demarcation line with eastern Poland, which had been occupied by the Soviets following the Ribbentrop-Molotov-Pact, also known as the German–Soviet Non-aggression Pact.

As part of the 4. Armee, StuGAbt 203 was subordinated to the 7. InfDiv by the beginning of May 1941. By 24 May, 2./StuGAbt 203 was commanded to the 268. InfDiv. The staff battery and 1. and 3./StuGAbt 203 were attached to the 7. InfDiv. The same day 2./203 moved into a new position in Waldlager 9b (forest camp). Both divisions were now accomodated in the forest camp and lay, well-disguised, side by side in the enormous woodland.

The organizational chart of VII. Armeekorps (under AOK 4, Heeresgruppe Mitte) dated 15 May shows clearly the subordinated units, among them the 7. and 268. InfDivs. Beside StuGAbt 203, various other smaller support units (signals, artillery and anti-aircraft, etc.) were available at Korps level.

By 31 May 1941 the commander of the 7. InfDiv gave new orders. According to the official jargon the division was responsible for border security, which was justified by a more and more hostile attitude of the Soviet Union towards Germany.

In case of a Soviet invasion, the codeword "Achtung Berta" would be given. It is not surprising that "Berta" and "Barbarossa" share the same first letter. All subunits of the 7. InfDiv were assigned exact locations to move into; StuGAbt 203, as the attached Sturmartillerie element, received orders to move to Trzcianka.

Shortly before the start of the invasion a marginally modified organizational structure, KStN 446 (Behelf) dated 1 April 1941, was implemented. In principle this "Behelf", or makeshift structure, followed the wish to provide the combat batteries with a seventh assault gun for the battery commanders. It is, however, not known whether StuGAbt 203 introduced this measure immediately. This would have required the delivery of at least three new Sturmgeschütze.

Deviating from the new structure, the Abteilung apparently decided autonomously to drop the platoon leaders' Führerwagen (le gep BeobKw, SdKfz 253). This measure

This soldier, possibly a 1. Lt, also wears the field-grey uniform of the assault gun crews. The standard shows the emblem of the Sturmgeschütz-Abteilung 203, the elephant.

was taken for reasonable tactical reasons. The half-tracked vehicles, which were only lightly armoured, made it impossible to effectively lead the battery from the front. Furthermore, their cross-country mobility was far inferior to that of the assault guns. Instead the platoon leaders now mounted one of their two Sturmgeschütze. This allowed the responsible NCOs to lead their platoon from the front. This measure improved the combat value of the platoons considerably and reduced both personnel and materiel losses and would become standard procedure with the next KStN 446 structure. It is however clear that not all Sturmgeschütz-Abteilungen implemented the April 1941 makeshift structure, one documented example being StuGAbt 185.

Oberleutnant (First Lieutenant) Hans Dostler, the chief of the 2./203 before the transfer to Poland. The officer wears the field grey uniform of the assault artillery. This resembled the black special clothing for tank crews, the field-grey colour camouflaged much better in the terrain. On his lapel, Dostler wears the Eisernes Kreuz II. Klasse ribbon, which had already been awarded to him during the French campaign.

Dostler's comrade, Lieutenant Hermann Conradt, also in Jüterbog in February 1941. After Dostler's death in August 1942, Conradt was to take over the command of the 2. Bttr.

4.

Armee Nachr. Rgt. 589.
Prop. Kp. 689.
Arko. 147.
10 cm Kan. Abt. I./109.
Verm. Abt. 501.
Verm. Zug d. Ob. Bau-St. 10.
Verm. Zug 701.
Druckereizug 20403

Kartenstelle 570.
Wetterpeilzug 506.
Pi. Rgt. Stab 516, 518, 674 (mit
   Nachsch. Kp. 435. (Pi))
Pi. Batl. 635 (mot) (mit Brüko
            635 (mot))
Ob. Bau Stab 10.

2./Pz. Jäg. Abt. 654 (3,7)

Kdr. d. Bautr. 6, 24, 33.
Bau Batl. 11, 97, 133, 213.
1 (techn.) Zug d. 7./Fest. Bau Batl. 40.
Str. Bau Batl. 544, 575, 584, 676 (o. 1. Kp.)
16 R. A. D. Abteilungen

Luftwaffe :
Koluft 4. mit Stabi a
Kurierstaffel 11.
Aufkl. St. 1. (H)/21.
  "   " 5. (H)/12.
  "   " 7. (H)/12.
  "   " 1. (H)/10.
  "   " 2. (H)/41.

 IX.   mit Korpstruppen und
Br. Bau Batl. 42.
Bau Batl. 222, 410.

 XXXXIII.   mit Korpstruppen und
Bau Batl. 24, 125.

 XXIV.   mit Korpstruppen und
Br. Bau Batl. 21.
Bau Batl. 136.
(beide für 255. J.D.)

 LIII.   mit Korpstruppen.

XIII.

Nachr. Abt. 53.
Arko. 44.
15 cm Kan. Abt. 740. (mot)
s. F. H. Abt. 422.
21 cm Mörser Abt. II./109. (mot)
Pz. Abt. (Flam.) 100.

4. 293. 137. 134.

Dazu: z.b.V. 442.

mit Heeres- u. Versorgungstruppen

für :
  a) A.O.K. 4.
  b) Fe. Stab 49.

VII.

Sich. 221. 258. 268.
23.   7.

Nachr. Abt. 47.
Arko. 7.
Artl. Rgt. Stab 41.
10 cm Kan. Abt. II./41 (mot)
s. F. H. Abt. II./43 (mot)
s. F. H. Abt. III./818 (mot)
Sturm Gesch. Abt. 203.
21 cm Mörser Abt. 736.
Beob. Abt. 7.
Bau Batl. 129, 217.
Flak Abt. II./14.

Höh. Kdo. XXXV.

292.
45.   252.

Nachr. Abt. 435.
Arko. 17.
Artl. Rgt. Stab 622 (mot)
gem. Artl. Abt. II./71, I./108 (mot-bedingt
              bewegl.)
Beob. Abt. 28.
Pz. Jäg. Abt. 654 (3,7) (o. 2. Kp.)
Br. Bau Batl. 577.
Pi. Batl. 752. (besp.)
Eisb. Pz. Zug 2.
Kdr. d. Bautr. 106.
Bau Batl. 17 [x], 134. [x]
7./(techn.) Fest. Bau Batl. 149.
4./Str. Bau Batl. 580.

XII.

131.   1. K.D.
263. 255. 78. 31.

Nachr. Abt. 52.
Arko. 112, 133, 139, 148.
Artl. Rgt. Stab 617, 697, 786 (mot)
10 cm Kan. Abt. 430, 709.
s. F. H. Abt. II./42, II./66, 101, 845.
Sturm Gesch. Abt. 192, 201.
Beob. Abt. 1 (o. Ballon Battr.), 8, 35.
V° Meßtrupp 504.
Pz. Jäg. Abt. 529 (4,7) (mot)
Fla. Batl. 610, 611.
Pi. Rgt. St. 413, 507, 513, 515.
Pi. Batl. 215, 750. (besp.)
Br. Bau Batl. 4, 593.
Kdr. d. Bautr. 40. [x]
Bau Batl. 9 [x], 46, 63 [x], 248 [x], 402.
7./(techn.) Fest. Bau Batl. 61, 152.
Flak Abt. I./26.

Organisation of the German 4. Armee on 15.05.1941

The Abteilung's command staff, also in Glogau. On the left of the picture stands OLt Behnke (Chief of Staff Battery), next to him is OLt Bausch. Without headgear the commander, Major Krokisius, is visible. To his left is the battalion doctor, Dr. Altvater.

After the beginning of Barbarossa, no photo showing the Zugführerwagen (SdKfz 253) is known. However, the numeration of the platoons was apparently not changed (see below). Consequently nine SdKfz 253 were saved but the fate of these vehicles is not known. Normally they would have been transferred to mobilize the forward observers of artillery units of infantry or tank divisions. After the start of the Russian campaign, however, such transfers were rather unlikely. Presumably, available vehicles were used by StuGAbt 203 as armoured radio posts.

The StuG units' initial tactical concept relied on lightly armoured ammunition carriers (le gep Mun Kw, SdKfz 252), which were part of the assault gun platoons. By May 1941, StuGAbt 203 had nine of these valuable vehicles available.

The delegation of single batteries of the battalion to other units such as infantry divisions caused problems. As an independent Abteilung, the unit had its own ammo and fuel transport, workshop and recovery services. While in the ideal case most supplies, such as food and fuel, could be provided by the divisions, these could not help with recovery and workshop services. They also lacked ammunition for the assault guns. Here, practicable solutions had to be found on a case-by-case basis.

When 2./203 was transferred to the 268. InfDiv, it had to be partly supplied over divisional borders. For this reason Major Krokisius disposed men and vehicles of the staff battery to the 2. Battery including parts of the workshop and a Bergezug (recovery team).

By April/May 1941, StuGAbt 203 introduced a system of markings to denote the vehicles. Sadly, so far no documents have been found proving the unit's exact practice. In order to give the batteries markings with distinctive colouring, most likely the German Army's standard order of precedence was adopted - white for 1. Bttr, red for 2. Bttr, yellow for 3. Bttr and finally green for StabsBttr. According to photos, the prominent elephant symbols, used on almost all vehicles, were painted in these colours, denoting their affiliation to the respective battery. Within the batteries, a system of one-digit numbering (battery staff) and two-digit numbering (combat platoons, ammo and combat train, and workshop section) was used.

The fact that practically all available WW II photos were in b/w makes a direct and veridical approach almost impossible. Any viewer of such images would normally recognize a bright marking on a dark grey vehicle base colour as being white. Having in mind the often poor quality of old photographic materials, differentiating between white and yellow would be difficult, or impossible. Since most photos seem to show bright markings, these would belong to either the 1. or 3. Bttr. Rather few photos show "darker" markings, which could denote 2. Bttr vehicles.

For the Stabsbatterie (staff battery) apparently no further colour was chosen but according to wartime photos it seems likely that white was chosen.

The Abteilung, like many Wehrmacht units, was equipped with a variety of different types of vehicles. In addition to fully off-road vehicles such as the le gl Kfz Stöwer (Kfz 2), standard rear-wheel drive passenger cars and an Opel Kadett can be seen here.

The three large 22 t low-bed trailers (SdAnh 116) each required a whole four-axle railway wagon (SSI 65). The loading of the long and wide trailers was difficult and required great caution. The cabin of the rear chassis driver was equipped with a weather protection hood.

Officers of the Abteilung, OLt Behnke and Bausch, Major Krokisius and Dr Altvater in a passenger wagon. In a few weeks the men were to exchange comfort for the reality of war.

During the Polish campaign, many bridges were destroyed in the defeated nation now called a General-Gouvernement. This one led across the Vistula near Leslau (Włocławek).

Towards the end of February, the Abteilung moved into accommodation in Brest-Kujawien (Brześć Kujawsk) near Leslau.

Parts of the Abteilung were housed in the buildings of the sugar factory in Brest-Kujawien. As a "guest gift", the director of the factory was given a ride in the assault gun.

With obvious pleasure, the director (wearing a steel helmet) occupied the loader's seat and hatch.

In the course of the ride, a tree was knocked down to demonstrate the power of the assault guns.

The officers and parts of the staff battery were comfortably housed in a mental hospital near Leslau.

Major Krokisius and another officer enjoy the last quiet days before the further transfer to the east.

Dr Altvater and OLt Behnke poring over paperwork. Here, Behnke is wearing the normal service uniform with shank boots.

The basic equipment of the StuG units included the "Führerwagen", the le gep BeobKw (SdKfz 253). These were intended to serve the battery leaders as light armoured command vehicles. Because of their low armour protection, they were not to be used at the front during combat operations, and the battery leaders were assigned assault guns instead.

Sturmgeschütz-Batterie
Actual organizational structure StuGAbt 203 as of May 1941
according KStN 446 dated 1 July 1940*

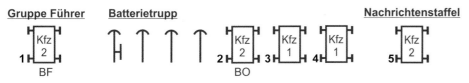

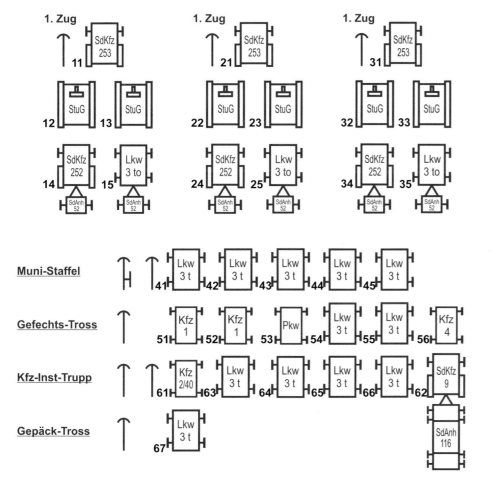

* Deployed as independent battery. Provision with recovery services. Identified tactical numbers in red. Changes in provision with motor vehiclue to supply situation.

Communication within the Sturmgeschütz-Abteilung

During the establishment of the German Army great emphasis was put on the development and introduction of effective radio communication. The leaders at every level would be able to contact their subordinate units in all situations and over tactical ranges. In this context the term "contact" must be more exactly defined. At the beginning of the war, communication channels were often one-sided depending on the command level. Orders could be given top down only and the recipient had no chance to confirm receipt of an order or report his own observations. This of course limited the units' range of applications considerably. A possible reason for this inadequate provision could have been materiel shortages. It is likely that the German procurement authorities were eager to solve these problems, but this would take time.

Principally, the Sturmartillerie used radios as mobile and short range communication equipment operating on different (artillery) frequencies from those of the Panzertruppe. The Abteilungsstab, however, depended on long range radio sets compatible with the radio equipment of the Panzertruppe or infantry divisions. Thus communication with higher level units and corps or army was ensured.

Short range communication

10 W S h
This VHF 10 W transmitter worked in the frequency band 23 to 25 MHz. According to the manual HDv 200/2m, it had a voice range of four to eight km Führerwagen to Führerwagen and two to four km Führerwagen to Sturmgeschütz. Ranges in morse were higher.

Ukw E h
The VHF receiver used the same frequency band.

Both radios used the 2 m rod antenna d.
Both devices were combined in sets. The Fu 15 radio set comprised only the Ukw E h receiver with peripheric components such as a converter. The Fu 16 radio set comprised the 10 W S h and the Ukw E h receiver plus peripheric parts.

Funkverbindungen einer Sturmbatterie (mots.)

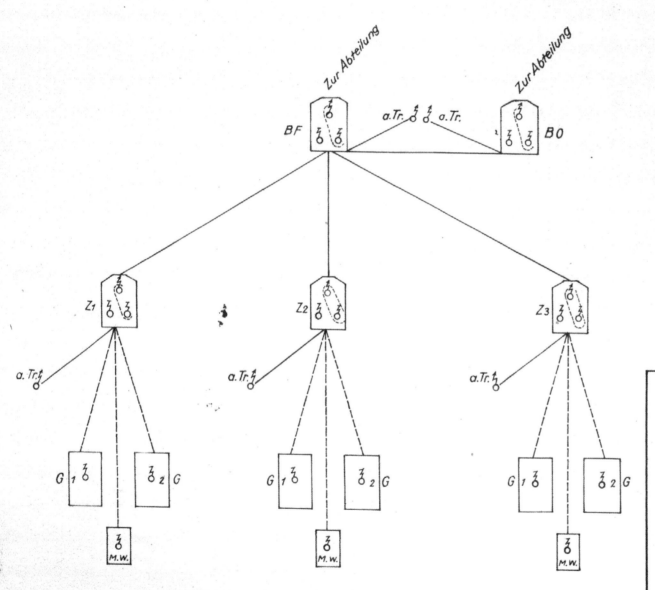

Erläuterungen:

BF – Batterieführer
BO – Beobachtungsoffizier
Z₁ – Zugführer 1 Zug
G – Geschütze
MW – Munitionswagen

FU 15 EU	Frequenzbereich
FU 16 SE 10U	23 74,95 MHz
FU 17 SEU	Skala Teilung
	240-280 1 Tlstr.- 50kHz

a.Tr.- abgesetzter Trupp

Mobile communication

The Torn FuG h was a portable transceiver working in the same frequency band. It was used by observers dismounted from the Führerwagen as a radio set. The Torn FuG h was part of the Fu 17 radio set. In the initial phase of the war the ammo carriers (SdKfz 252) apparently also used this transceiver.

Long range communication

30 W S
This medium wave 30 W transmitter worked in the frequency band 1 to 3 MHz. It had a voice range of 40 km. Range in morse was higher.

Mw E c
The medium wave receiver used the same frequency band.

Both devices were combined in the Fu 8 radio set with the necessary peripheric components. The 30 W S would normally use a frame antenna as issued to the Kfz 17.

Distribution of radio sets in the Sturmgeschütz-Abteilung as of April 1941

The idealized table page 34 shows the principal provision with radio sets within the StuGBttr (or Sturmbatterie) with its three platoons. The six Sturmgeschütze and the three Muniwagen (le gep MunKw, SdKfz 252) were issued with Fu 15 radio sets only. These radios were mere receivers, thus they were not able to transmit. A platoon's Führerwagen (le gep BeobKw, SdKfz 253), being standard at that time, had a full provision with Fu 15 and Fu 16 sets, allowing the platoon leaders to keep in full contact with their platoons. Using the two receivers it was possible to monitor incoming calls from the battery commanders or the various combat troop units (superior units) at the same time.

At around the end of 1941 (the exact date is unknown) each Sturmgeschütz was issued with Fu 16 instead of Fu 15 allowing more effective two-way communication.

The platoon leader could dismount one man as a forward observer. Contact was kept using the Fu 17 portable transceiver. If the platoon leader used one of the two StuGs, the additional Fu 16 had to be installed in the assault gun. The exact installation details of the radios and converters is unknown; the early StuG versions' (Ausf A to D) superstructure had only one armoured bay and so the installation of the radios in the cramped interior would have been possible only with problems.

The Batterietrupp (battery HQ section) had two further Führerwagen (SdKfz 253) with identical radio equipment for the Batteriechef and the Batterieoffizier (commander and his deputy). A Kfz 15 could substitute the Führerwagen.

When platoon leaders mounted Sturmgeschütze, Fu 16s were also installed. By late 1941 a seventh Sturmgeschütz was issued to the batteries replacing the battery commander's Führerwagen and this was also fitted with Fu 15 and Fu 16 sets.

On the battalion level, the Abteilungs-Kommandeur would rely on equivalent 30 W S Funktrupps (radio sections) mounted in a Kfz 15 or 17 or respective substitutions. Having in mind the limitations given by the radio ranges of the Sturmgeschütz batteries' 10 W S h transmitter, any separation of the battalion elements was problematic. If one battery was subordinated to a different infantry or tank division, contact with the mother unit was jeopardized.

Vehicles of the 2./StuGAbt 203 at Glogów station during transport to the east. The 3 t truck with the number 37 was equipped with a closed wooden body - the field kitchen was accommodated here. The le gl Pkw (light cross country car) with the number 32 is a leichter Truppenluftschutzwagen (light air defence vehicle); it carries two MG 34s in a twin base mount.

This Sturmgeschütz also belonged to the 2. Bttr; the number "32" identifies it as the 2nd vehicle of the 3rd platoon. Unlike the tank units, many StuG divisions provided their assault guns with lamp guard solutions of very different design.

This Obergefreiter demonstrates the operation of the radios in an SdKfz 253. Above are the two components of the Fu 16 equipment set (Ukw E h, 10 W S h). A 20 W S c is mounted below. Normal for assault artillery would be the 30 W S a.

Furthermore, a portable radio was part of the equipment of the "Führerwagen". This field radio (FeldFu h, range 1.5km), here operated by a soldier of the Waffen-SS, was not assigned until 1942/43.

Originally, each assault gun was to receive only one Ukw receiver h (Fu 15 equipment set). Under the device the transformer can be seen. This ensured only one-way communication. The platoon leaders in their "Führerwagen" additionally received an Fu 16 set of equipment (10 W transmitter as well as a Ukw E h receiver). An on-board intercom system was not to be installed until later; in this Ausf E the commander still has a speaking tube at his disposal.

While the commander had a headset, the gunner listened to the radio traffic through a loudspeaker.

Later, the assault guns received an Fu 16 radio set, which was operated by the gunner. Again, the transformers are located close to the radio transmitter or receiver.

B-TAG
THE ELEPHANTS
GO TO WAR

CHAPTER 3

While the le gep BeobKw (SdKfz 253) was soon withdrawn from its intended use, the le gep MunKw (SdKfz 252) ammunition vehicle remained in service. Each battery had three of these useful vehicles, one per platoon.

JUNE 1941

For many reasons, the German General Staff postponed the planned invasion of the Soviet Union several times. The beginning of the attack was given the codename B-Tag, or Berta-Tag, (B more correctly standing for "Barbarossa"). Preparations for the invasion were disguised as exercises for a counterattack against possible Soviet aggression towards the Reich.

However, some days before B-Tag, the General Staff let the cat out of the bag when higher level staffs were informed of Hitler's real plans. An entry in the VII. Armeekorps war diary, dated 1 June 1941, states:

On B-Tag the "deutsche Ostheer" (German Army in the East) will attack to annihilate Bolshevism and the Red Army in order to thwart any Soviet attempts to join the side of our enemies...

While the staff of the VII. Armeekorps gave clear tactical missions to its subordinated divisions and the divisional artillery, StuGAbt 203 was not addressed, possibly because the unit was too small or because it was already clearly subordinated.

By 21 June, the 7. InfDiv gave its daily order:

Soldiers of the 7. Division!
The Führer has given the command for the attack...

At dusk on 21 June, Abteilung 203 was put on full alert. After refueling and a last maintenance, Major Krokisius read out the declaration of war against the Soviet Union and the tactical orders issued by Heeresgruppe Mitte.

Heeresgruppe Mitte was given Moscow as their prime target. On the way to the Russian capital a number of interim goals were set. After the crossing of the River Bug, the VII. Armeekorps would approach and take Bialystok.

Subordination Chart 22 June 1941
HG Mitte, AOK 4, VII. AK
Staff battery, 1. and 3./StuGAbt 203 to 7. InfDiv.
2./StuGAbt 203 to 268. InfDiv

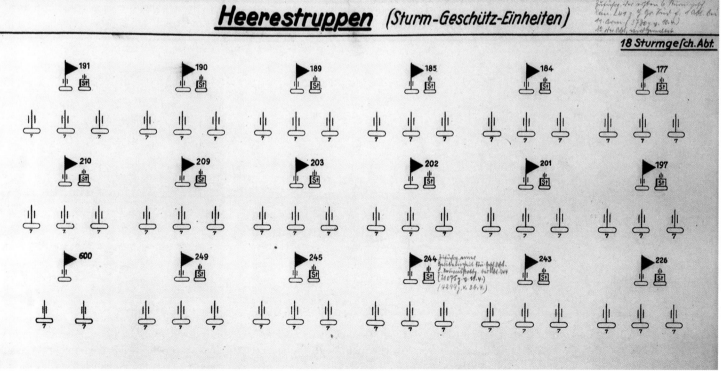

Heerestruppen (Sturm-Geschütz-Einheiten)

This assault gun failed in action with a damaged idler wheel. The damage could apparently not be repaired so recovery was ordered by the recovery platoon. Interestingly, the vehicle number "33" was also painted on the rear wall of the fighting compartment.

Dr. Altvater, the Abteilung's physician, used an s gl Pkw (o), Kfz 1. This particular vehicle was a Wanderer W 11. The green elephant symbol refers to the Stabsbatterie (staff battery).

Assault guns of 1./StuGAbt 203 form up for the attack on Russian positions near Smolensk. The car of the battery commander, OLt Josef Freiherr von Gleichenstein, with the tactical number "2" can be seen in the centre.

Rest in a village near Smolensk. The equipment of the Abteilung with cars and trucks was quite mixed; due to the lack of standardisation in German industry there was a great variety of types. The detachment also had commercially available cars like this Opel Olympia. The truck on the right is a Faun L 600, which probably did not belong to StuGAbt 203.

A further physician of the Abteilung, Dr. Gärtner, stands near a brand-new BeiKrad (motorcycle with sidecar). The Wehrmacht used motorbikes from a bewilderingly large number of different manufacturers. This machine was assigned to the medical section of 1. Bttr.

The battalion doctor, Dr. Altvater, had "organized" a waterproof felt cape from a cattle herder in the summer of 1941. The equipment of the German units in 1941 was not appropriate for the Russian climate. This was to become painfully apparent with the onset of winter.

The 3. platoon of a battery of StuGAbt 203. The le gep MunKw was primarily used to transport ammunition under enemy fire, but was also used for other goods such as fuel and rations. Their armour protected the vehicles against light infantry fire.

The field kitchen was mounted on a 3 t Opel Blitz 3,6-36 S truck. The special superstructure was made by the detachment itself during its deployment in Jüterbog.

In addition to two assault guns, each assault gun platoon originally had two ammunition vehicles, a le gep MunKw (SdKfz 252) and a conventional 3 t truck. Both vehicles had light ammunition trailers SdAnh 32, which had space for 64 7.5 cm shells.

The ambulance trucks in Jüterbog have also been provisionally converted for the care of the wounded.

The vehicles of Sturmgeschütz-Abteilung 203 were well camouflaged in the forest camp near Małkinia Górna, hidden against observation. The men of the division were not informed about the attack on the Soviet Union until the very end.

The twin battles for Byalistok and Minsk

The war diaries of the infantry divisions give little information on the combat of StuGAbt 203. A good source, however, are the reminiscences of Friedrich Gassauer and Heinz Angelmeier, who published a short essay in the newsletter of the "Gemeinschaft der Sturmartillerie".

1./StuGAbt 203

The first battery supported elements of the 7. InfDiv during combat against the newly established Soviet border fortifications. The bunkers defending the railway line to Bialystok near Szulborze were destroyed by fire from the Sturmgeschütze and divisional artillery; engineers took care of the rest. Since the Soviets were absolutely surprised, no organized defence at the line of bunkers could be established. Thus the assault guns effectively pushed forward the advance of the infantry.

3./StuGAbt 203

Attached to InfRgt 19 of the 7. InfDiv, the battery lost its commander, ObLt Wirth and his battery officer Lt Bausch; both fell during the first day of combat.

2./StuGAbt 203

By 23 June at 6.00 hours the 268. InfDiv established an advance party consisting of a bicycle company, four StuG from 2./203 and two AT gun platoons to advance east to Domanovo. The town was taken without resistance. By 14.30 InfRgt 568 reported that an assault gun had broken through a wooden bridge. Parts of the bicycle company, which already succeeded in crossing the river, entrenched to protect the gun. Engineers of 2./PiBtl 268 were called upon. With the help of the engineers, the Sturmgeschütz was brought back on track.

After two days the separation of StuGAbt 203 created the first problems. While the bulk of the Abteilung was in the 7. InfDiv's combat sector, 3./StuGAbt 203 was subordinated to the division's right neighbor, the 268. InfDiv. Thus the battery drifted away due to divisional orders, making contact with the mother unit difficult. Thus all supply had to be provided by the 268. InfDiv, resulting in great initial difficulties. The operational readiness of the Sturmgeschütze was endangered due to missing spare parts and workshop services.

Winker trowel in hand, the unit commander, Major Krokisius, instructs his assault guns. Infantry officers stand at his side. In a relatively small unit (division/battalion), the commander's personal example was important – his place was in front.

The two remaining batteries supported InfRgt 51 and 52 of the 7. InfDiv. The infantry advance was escorted at the vanguard. Soviet counterattacks were described as being aimless and poorly led. Despite this fact, the 7. InfDiv reported by 23 June the loss of ten AT guns and bloody personnel losses during that day.

By 25 June, the division reported all enemy counterattacks as being repulsed. More than 100 tanks had been destroyed. On this day the unit and StuGAbt 203 crossed the River Narev, a tributary to the River Bug, using the railway bridge which was not destroyed by enemy forces.

The advance was pushed forward in the direction of Grodno. On the way, the 7. InfDiv turned south towards Bialystok together with further forces of the VII. AK. Four days later, by 29 June, the pocket around Bialystok was closed and the battle of encirclement started.

Each battery had a le gep MunKw (SdKfz 252) and a 3 t munitions truck. These three trucks (numbers 15, 25 and 35) are shown here. Each truck carries an SdAnh 32 with 64 7.5 cm grenades.

At the beginning of the attack, parts of a Panzerjäger Abteilung with Panzerjäger I cross the Bug over a railway bridge. Assault guns of Abteilung 203 follow close behind. This photo was taken by the driver of an assault gun out of his visor.

Wherever possible, fords were used to cross watercourses. There was always the danger of heavy vehicles getting stuck in the soggy ground. Here, infantry on a le gep MunKw (SdKfz 252) use the opportunity to cross with dry feet.

These assault guns of the 1./StuGAbt 203 cross the River Bug over a pioneer bridge. This pontoon bridge (Brückengerät B) had a capacity of 4 to 24 t, depending on the length. Used as a ferry, tanks weighing up to 60 t could cross.

The application of the elephant symbol varied slightly from battery to battery. For the most part, it is only clearly visible on vehicles belonging to the 1. Bttr as it was applied in white paint. This assault gun of the 1./StuGAbt 203 was photographed in the forest camp near Małkinia Górna in eastern Poland, shortly before the attack on Russia began.

It was not possible to equip the Abteilung purely with 3 t trucks of one manufacturer. Besides Opel Blitz, Borgward trucks of the type 3 t Benzin GW were also assigned. These trucks belonged to the staff battery as ambulances. On the driver's cab, fascines were stowed, which were helpful on damp ground.

Vehicles of the Abteilung are overtaken by a Panzerjäger-Kompanie with 3.7 cm PaK. It seems to be raining, not unusual for the Russian summer. The assault gun was covered with the rain cover. These are soon to be lost in hard use.

Russia had only a rudimentary transport network. Therefore, the railway embankments of the broad-gauge railway were used as often as possible as a road substitute. Here, parts of the Elefanten-Abteilung (elephant battalion) are on the move.

Major Krokisius studying a map with the commander of the 7. InfDiv, Lieutenant General Eccard Freiherr von Gablenz. Parts of the Elefanten-Abteilung were subordinated to his infantry division during the double battle for Byalistock and Minsk.

The assistant doctor of StuGAbt 203 near the cauldron of Byalistok in July 1941. The unit was partially equipped with commercial passenger cars (Kfz 1). These pre-war rear-wheel-drive designs were not suitable for use on the Eastern Front, despite their high ground clearance.

The Stöwer-built le gl Pkw (E) on "Einheitsfahrgestell für leichte Pkw" – the standard chassis for light passenger cars – was a purposeful development and, thanks to all-wheel drive and four-wheel steering, extremely capable off-road. This vehicle was also equipped as Kfz 4 with two MG 34 in ZwiSoLa. Due to the complicated chassis, these vehicles wore out quickly.

One tractor was not enough to tow the KW. The appearance of the heavy tanks, as well as the T-34, was a shock for the armoured troops and the assault artillery, who were used to success.

In the summer of 1941, German troops were to encounter heavy tanks of the KW type (here an M 40 with additional armour) for the first time. This tank was captured by the 267. InfDiv, recognizable by the crossed horse heads on the gun shield. An s ZgKw 18t (SdKfz 9) of Abt 203 tows the apparently undamaged tank.

Major Krokisius and his adjutant OLt Bausch in a moment of calm. In the field, only tents were available for accommodation.

The assault guns, like all armoured vehicles, required regular maintenance. This soldier demonstrates lifting a running wheel using the jack and a special tool. The latter was inserted into the holes of the running wheels to provide an attachment point.

These three soldiers were awarded the Eisernes Kreuz II. Klasse during the battles for Smolensk. The medal was worn on the ribbon on the day of the award. Later, the white-red-white ribbon alone indicated the honour.

The car of the battery officer of one of the three batteries on an advance road. The wrecks of Russian columns line the road. This one was also initially equipped with a heavy commercial passenger car (s Pkw (o), or Kfz 1).

JULY 1941

Advance to the river Beresina

By 4 July, StuGAbt 203 was transferred to LIII. AK where the unit was attached to the 52. InfDiv. Hampered by the poorly developed road network, it took some days to reach the new destination.

Subordination Chart 4 July 1941,
HG Mitte, AOK 4, LIII. AK
StuGAbt 203 attached to 52. InfDiv

Following the 52. InfDiv, StuGAbt 203 advanced via Slonim, Sluzk and Minsk to Borrisov. During this raid the Sturmgeschütze covered great distances; the drivers were heavily strained in long day and night marches. Finally the River Dnieper was reached south of Orsha.

Referring to Gassauer's and Engelmeier's reminiscences, the Abteilung used the tactical concept of dismounted observers for the first time during this commitment. The NCOs accompanied the infantry and kept contact with the Abteilung using portable transceivers (Torn FuG h). Apparently this approach never worked satisfactorily because it proved impossible to lead the combat of Sturmgeschütze by officers attached to forward infantry forces. The battery commander's own armoured observation vehicle (le gep BeobKw, SdKfz 253) was indispensable despite its light armour (the battery leaders were not issued with Sturmgeschütz while the platoon leaders were mounted on their two assault guns). Furthermore, it became standard procedure to send the battery officer to the infantry battalion staff. Being an experienced assault artillery officer, he had the task to advise the commanding officers about his unit's possibilities. A strong personality was needed to reject orders from superior officers which overtaxed or entirely endangered his unit.

Subordination Chart 12 July 1941
HG Mitte, AOK 4, LIII. AK
1./StuGAbt 203 attached to 29. InfDiv

On their advance eastwards, the German attackers encountered the Stalin Line. This defensive line was established on the western borders of the Soviet Union from 1929. Before Minsk, the assault guns of StuGAbt 203 were called in to fight the bunkers.

By 12 July, 1./203 was attached to the advance party of the 29. InfDiv. This division was part of the forces advancing to the city of Smolensk. By 16 July the battery attacked and entered the outskirts. Heavy street fighting took place, a situation tanks and assault guns would normally avoid. In the confusing network of streets and buildings, intact or destroyed, the doggedly fighting Soviet troops could easily find good firing positions.

Due to their inadequate observation means, Sturmgeschütz commanders were forced to drive into combat with open hatches. A further reason for this practice was that most tankers favoured being able to hear the noises of battle directly so, in a a sense, this was certainly a psychological problem. This could, however, end fatally since the Soviets quickly learned to take advantage of this fact. During the battle of Smolensk Geschützführer (assault gun cdr) Lt Müller was severely wounded by a hand grenade which was thrown into his open hatch.

Smolensk was taken by 22 July, leaving only a few pockets of resistance.

In this situation the complete 1. Bttr fell ill with heavy diarrhoea. A short phase of recovery was ordered from 28 to 30 July. The battery remained in Smolensk until mid August, clearing the city of single, and still resisting, Russian soldiers.

During this phase the Soviets launched several counterattacks supported by artillery and air raids.

Assault guns of the 1./StuGAbt 203 on the advance towards Smolensk, July 1941. During a technical stop, engines, oil levels and fuel supply are checked. This work was essential so that the vehicles would not fail due to technical problems in the event of a surprise deployment.

Men of StuGAbt 203 eating; a metal grate serves as a barbecue. In the background is a Kfz 4 Truppenluftschutz-Kraftwagen (TrLuftschKw, air defence vehicle) based on the le gl passenger car "Stöwer". This vehicle was equipped with two MG 34s in a twin-mount (ZwiSoLa) which was used to defend against low-flying aircraft.

StuGAbt 203 was equipped with a number of light and heavy motorbikes. The versatile light vehicles were used for reconnaissance and liaison duties. These vehicles were not up to the conditions in Russia. The soldiers are wearing normal field uniforms.

An assault gun of the 2./StuGAbt 203. The vehicle has been parked under trees in an exemplary manner. A frame has been placed on the engine deck to provide secure support for spare chain links and rollers. The cramped fighting compartment forced the crews to stow all personal belongings outside.

The propaganda company on the ground. A soldier makes audio recordings of a (posed!) service briefing. On the right is the battalion commander, Major Krokisius, in the middle Lt Metzger, platoon leader in the 1. Bttr and to the left OLt Freiherr von Gleichenstein (Chef 1./203).

Geschütz No "23" of the 1. Bttr. The assault gun shows a good score on the gun mantlet – eight white lines. In front of the casemate superstructure is the removed protective cap of the 7.5 cm StuK L/24.

On 1 August, the Abteilung marched into Roslavl, a larger town south of Smolensk. Behind the town shield, one of the battalion´s four Truppen-Luftschutzwagen (AA Kfz 4 protection vehicles) is visible, the two MG 34s are not mounted.

During the attack on Smolensk, T-34s appeared in larger numbers for the first time. The men in their assault guns were greatly shocked, as the tank could hardly be engaged with the 7.5 cm StuK L/24. This otherwise undamaged Model 41 with a 76.2 mm F-34 was abandoned by the crew after the loss of the left track.

Parts of the Abteilung's recovery section, in front an s ZgKw 18 t (SdKfz 9) with low-bed trailer (SdAnh 116), in Roslavl. The vehicles were pulled under trees - the Russian air force could always strike. The road is paved and lined with telegraph lines. Possibly, this is the main connecting road to Smolensk.

A short rest on the way to Smolensk. The photo was taken near Roslavl. The crew, two privates and a non-commissioned officer, are wearing the field-grey Sonderuniform (special uniform). Gun No "22" probably belonged to the 1. Bttr.

The crew of this Sturmgeschütz enjoys the peace and quiet between the combat missions. The improvised lamp guard, which was retrofitted to the assault guns of the original equipment of Abteilung 203, is clearly visible.

The low height of the assault guns made concealment in the terrain easy. Surprise attacks were mostly successful. This vehicle of the 1./StuGAbt 203 shows the white elephant and the typical lamp guard fitted to the vehicles.

AUGUST 1941

While the 1. Bttr remained in Smolensk, the 2. and 3./203 were attached to the 197. InfDiv (VII. AK). By 21 July the bulk of the Abteilung moved towards Roslavl, again a distance of more than 100 km. 1./203 would remain in Smolensk until 14 August, when it followed up to Roslavl.

The city was attacked by elements of the 23. InfDiv (reinforced by StuGAbt 203) and the 4. PzDiv. According to the 23. InfDiv., the 4. PzDiv had to deal with its own problems and followed with a delay of several days. Roslavl was taken by 3 August.

Subordination Chart
30 August 1941, HG Mitte, VII. AK
StuGAbt 203 to 23. InfDiv

Angelmeier remembers that Soviet Rata dive bombers were continuously flying attacks, dropping many "eggs" on the attacking German forces. Most of these outdated planes were downed by German fighters or AA artillery.

At the River Desna the German advance came to a short halt. By 14 August StuGAbt 203 submitted a monthly report while the unit was subordinated to the VII. Armeekorps. According to this report the unit had to lament the death of two NCOs and four enlisted men. On the materiel side, the Abteilung lost one Sturmgeschütz, two trucks, one passenger car and three motorcycles. Besides the sheer figures, the commander's judgement is interesting:

Despite the personnel losses, the Abteilung is fully combat ready. Only 1/3 of the Sturmgeschütze are operational. 2/3 suffer from of worn out engines, which have considerably exceeded their normal service life. Only 1/3 of the engines could be replaced or overhauled. The stock of spare parts is sufficient to get 50% combat ready within a short time. With delivery of new engines and engine spare parts a 100 % combat readiness can be achieved.

A month later, the unit reported further materiel losses: seven motorcycles and two ammunition trailers. The commander complained about the missing personnel replacements and the inadequate supply of spare parts and optical equipment.

A final assessment of the first days of combat of StuGAbt 203 is not possible. All available war diaries and files of the concerned army corps and divisions were carefully checked. It is worth mentioning that the combat of the Sturmgeschütz-Abteilungen involved here (Abt 177, 191, 192, 201 and 203) was not particularly emphasized. The reason for this might be the fact that the Abteilungen were normally split up, often with only one or two platoons attached to single regiments. These secondments were possibly too small to mention.

On 30 August the Soviets launched a counteroffensive passing the city of Yelnya to both the north and south. In terms of men, far superior forces broke though the German lines and forced back the entire XXXXVII. AK. For the first time in the Ostfeldzug (eastern campaign) Soviet units had regained control over Russian territory.

In this situation the VII. Armeekorps turned its direction of attack to the north towards Vyasma. Reinforced by StuGAbt 203, the 23. InfDiv was one of the units defending positions at the River Desna, at the southern flank of the Russian breakthrough. All enemy attempts to stop this advance near Roslavl failed. Following this setback the so far successful Soviet attack at Yelnya collapsed.

Subordination Chart 30 August 1941
HG Mitte, VII. AK
StuGAbt 203 attached to 297. InfDiv

Lt Metzger of 1./203 led his platoon into combat. By evening, 23 enemy tanks were destroyed and for this, Metzger was awarded the Ritterkreuz. By 1 September, 3./203 assisted an attack by InfRgt 497 and subsequently a further six enemy tanks were destroyed. Gun no. "12" burnt down after a direct hit; the Geschützführer Uffz Weisshaupt was wounded. Sturmgeschütz "32" was also hit, forcing the crew to abandon it.

After some days of sorely needed recovery, the unit was attached to the pioneers of the 23. InfDiv, assisting them in clearing woodland occupied by Russian soldiers.

By that time all German units were obliged to submit reports (Zustands-berichte) on a regular basis. The extent and quality of these reports changed over time. By 1941 monthly reports describing the unit´s losses of men and materiel over this given period were the norm. The commander concluded his report by giving his personal judgment of the situation. However, although helpful for a historian, the information contained in them is rather scant.

The IX. Armeekorps´ war diary gives a noteworthy entry for 12 August:
Leaving behind motor vehicles

The workshop company of a division left behind 18 motor vehicles which could not be taken along during the advance. A rearguard was not deployed; instead an elderly country woman was commissioned to guard the vehicle park. This irresponsible conduct resulted in the theft of 10 motor vehicles; the rest were completely cannibalized. We again point out that any transfer of vehicles to workshop units or collection points must be done on the basis of receipts. It is vital that troops guard these collection points.

If major work had to be done in the engine compartment of the assault gun, the Heckpanzer (rear armour) had to be removed. If suitable equipment such as the Kfz 100 was available, this was unproblematic. Since these vehicles were never available in the necessary numbers StuGAbt 203 built improvised cranes, which were quite sufficient, onto their heavy tractors.

A battery of StuGAbt 203 is getting ready for action. In addition to assault guns, a le gep MunKw (SdKfz 252) can be seen in the dust at the rear.

This 3./203 assault gun (the colour of the elephant is presumably yellow) obviously has severe running gear damage. The second and fifth running wheels are ripped, either by shelling or a mine. In the course of a dynamic forward attack, the workshop section was responsible for the quick repair of such problems.

An assault gun at full speed. The early variants could reach top speeds of up to 70 km/h. In order to preserve materiel, a more robust gearbox was installed with the Ausf C, and the speed was now limited to 40 km/h.

As those elephant symbols painted in red or yellow are not clearly recognizable on b/w pictures, this vehicle may belong to the 2. or 3. battery. The number "2" indicates the battery chief; the battery officer used a Kfz 15 with the number "1".

The wreck allows a view of the mounting points of the thin sloped steel sheets that were attached to the tank superstructure. The right sprocket has already been dismantled and will continue to be used. The photo was taken on the Desna during the advance on Smolensk.

Completely destroyed tanks or assault guns, which could not be repaired, served as spare-part donors. Here a mechanic is looking for usable parts in the engine compartment.

SEPTEMBER 1941

Subordination Chart 3 September 1941
HG Mitte, AOK 4, IX. AK
2./StuGAbt 203 attached to 137. InfDiv

At the beginning of September, 2./203 was attached to the 137. InfDiv. This subordination was cancelled by 6 September.

By 2 September the Russians launched a further counterattack. Two rifle divisions and one tank corps attacked the left flank of the VII. Armeekorps over the River Desna. The 10. PzDiv, 267. InfDiv and 23 InfDiv repelled the enemy, restoring the old main line of resistance. Further attacks by a rifle division against the 197. InfDiv were also repulsed. The Korps counted 173 destroyed tanks.

By 7 September StuGAbt 203 was withdrawn from service and a longer rest period followed. The unit recovered with generous allocations of food and alcoholic beverages helping the men to forget the war for a few precious moments. The complete unit received vaccines against cholera.

During this period the unit made a reconnaissance raid to recover the destroyed Sturmgeschütz "32". Supported by workshop elements, the assault gun was brought back to the unit.

Subordination Chart 23 September 1941
HG Mitte, AOK 4, VII. AK
2./StuGAbt 203 attached to various divisions

The crew of an assault gun eating somewhere outside Smolensk near Bogdanovka. The weather seems to be slowly getting worse, coats and scarves have been put on. On the left is an Unterwachtmeister, in the middle two Oberkanoniere and on the right a Gefreiter.

The construction of bridges was the responsibility of the pioneer battalions. If the combat troops had to help themselves, it could quickly end in disaster. This assault gun of the 1. Bttr broke through a wooden construction that was not able to withstand the weight of 20 tons. The vehicle itself seems undamaged.

On 7 September 1941, Lieutenant Eugen Metzger, (platoon leader in the 1. Bttr, was awarded the Eisernes Kreuz II. Klasse. The soldier wears the field-grey Sonderbekleidung - the jacket is closed. The medal was only worn openly on the day of its award, otherwise a white-red-white ribbon in the buttonhole indicated this honour.

In larger towns behind the front, the army group or army organised hygiene facilities. The "Bade-Entwesungsanstalt" served to combat epidemics and vermin; here the soldiers were deloused.

A certain degree of hygiene was also expected in the field. Private Dyck shaves with the simplest of means – a small mirror and wet pack are on the track cover.

A leichter gepanzerter Munitionskraftwagen (light armoured ammunition vehicle, SdKfz 252) crosses the Moskva on a simple wooden plank bridge. A sidecar motorbike of the Abteilung follows.

OCTOBER 1941

The battles of Vyasma and Bryansk

> **Subordination Chart 2 October 1941**
> HG Mitte, AOK 4, VII.AK
> StuGAbt 203 attached to 23. Inf-Div

By 29 September major parts of Heeresgruppe Mitte launched the planned attack towards Vyasma and Bryansk. The German units rushed through both cities, then split into a northern and a southern part. The northern part closed the ring around Vyasma.

On 14 October, the Moskva was reached at Borodino. The branched river system offered shallow fords that could be waded through by the assault guns. In the front assault gun OLt Haubner and soldiers Pauer and Glissmann can be seen.

By 2 October StuGAbt 203 was alerted and called to combat again as part of the VII. Armeekorps. The unit was heading for Vyasma. The 3./203, reinforced by a platoon of PzAbwAbt 23, was ordered to attack as an advance party towards the River Desna. During the advance one Sturmgeschütz hit a mine, killing StuG commander Uffz Weisshaupt.

On 5 October the advance party was attacked and several soldiers were wounded.

A week later the unit was again ordered to comb through dense and extensive forests to clear them of Russian soldiers who had been left behind. Despite the lack of suitable equipment and arms, the men of 203 had to be deployed here in an infantry role, escorting the slowly advancing assault guns.

By 10 October Heeresgruppe Mitte distributed pamphlets describing how to defeat the Russian T-34 tank to all units fighting at the front. For the Sturmgeschütz (and

The Rasputitza, the mud period, made it much more difficult for the German attackers to advance. Even crossing small watercourses could fail. This commander looks down skeptically while more assault guns wait in the background.

the PzKpfw IV), it was suggested to attack the hull sides with 7.5 cm GrPatr 38, the HE round.

Around 10 October the first snow fell. The staff of AOK 4 (4. Army) reported this change in weather conditions:

> *The present weather and road conditions, and the enemy's manner of fighting (resistance with focal points on roads, destruction of traffic routes and bridges, disguised deployment of snipers and heavy tanks) require an adjustment of our combat tactics…*
>
> *…*
>
> *Both the infantry and motorized infantry have to be mobilized at any costs…*
>
> *…*
>
> *Heavy weapons and ammunition must be transported by Panje-wagons (small horse carts) or carrier columns (POWs)…*
>
> *…*
>
> *As far as the road condition allows, the infantry must be given sufficient attachments of artillery, assault guns, tanks and 8.8 cm FlaK…*
>
> *…*
>
> *Antitank defence:*
> *The antitank defence has to face the commitment of heavy and super heavy tanks, which are immune to our AT guns and mines. The spearheads must be provided with single 10 cm guns and heavy AA guns…*

On 14 October the battle for Vyasma came to an end. The HQ of the XXXXVI. PzK gave notice that 100,000 POWs had been captured together with more than 900 guns and 140 AT guns. In addition, 100 tanks had been captured or destroyed.

It is again interesting to note that, contrary to popular belief, this report does not emphasize the Sturmgeschütze's ability to fight even heavy tanks. The obvious reason for this is the fact that the number of StuG units was still relatively low.

By 20 October the Abteilung was detached from the 23. InfDiv and moved to Vyasma. Five days later, by 25 October, the Abteilung received orders to move towards Moshaisk at the motorway Smolensk-Moscow. Great parts of the Soviet forces had been withdrawn after the Vyasma disaster to reinforce defensive positions at Moscow so the Sturmgeschü-

tze met very little resistance. The weather, however, worsened. After the heavy rainfall of *Rasputitsa*, the roads and open fields became bottomless "seas of mud".

Most motorized vehicles were impeded by the mud. Although tracked vehicles could partially maintain mobility, all supply collapsed. The longer the tracked vehicles had to move through this quagmire the more their drive trains and engines became dangerously overstressed.

The first winter storm impeded the march of all elements of StuGAbt 203. While the Sturmgeschütze could maintain their mobility within certain limits, all other vehicles had already met their limit. Under these conditions most cross county cars and trucks broke down and the delivery of replacements was not possible.

Following the thoroughfare, the Abteilung reached Moshaisk by 25 October and one day later Rusa was reached. Frequent Soviet bombing raids led to further casualties. Sadly, no files are known reporting the number of tank kills or the exact losses of StuGAbt 203. Basically StuG units could request delivery of new materiel, but were tied to certain conditions. A document of the IX. Armeekorps dated 19 October pointed out the correct procedure:

> *Requests for new Sturmgeschütze*
>
> *Because of the great demand every unit should be aware that requests can be complied with only partially by deliveries of new assault guns from the manufacturer or from general refurbishing facilities. We again have to point out that every inoperable Sturmgeschütz has to be recovered and must be sent back to Heereszeugamt (HZA, army depot) Magdeburg as soon as possible, as this affects the new delivery significantly. Any request has to be submitted in duplicate to the OKH, and must contain the following specifications:*
>
> *— Chassis number of the broken down Sturmgeschütz.*
> *— Position of the failed Sturmgeschütz.*
> *— As long as the StuG is not recovered the location must be given, if possible with a sketch.*
> *— If Sturmgeschütze have already been recovered, the relevant office must be indicated.*

Sudden thaws further complicated the defensive battles in the spring of 1942. This assault gun got stuck while trying to cross a stream. Russian peasants were forced to dig the vehicle out of the mud using the simplest of means. The vehicle itself shows severe damage – the housing of the recuperator is missing.

— If Sturmgeschütze were already sent back via train, time and location of shipment must be given…"

This interesting excerpt gives a brief insight to the army´s bureaucracy and logistics. Sadly, so far little is known regarding the number of armoured vehicles sent back to the Reich for general overhaul.

Subordination Chart 17 October 1941
HG Mitte, AOK 4, Panzergruppe 4
2./StuGAbt 203 attached to 78. InfDiv

Subordination Chart 25 October 1941
HG Mitte, AOK 4, Panzergruppe 4
StuGAbt 203 attached to 78. and 87. InfDiv

The equipment of all German formations, including the assault gun units, was heavily affected by the tense production situation in the Reich. The factories were not able to deliver the necessary quantities of soft-skinned vehicles and artillery tractors. Although the valid organizational standards authorized cross-country cars in all essential established posts, the "small print" in the KStN allowed alternative deliveries. So, instead of issuing le or m gl Pkw (leichte or mittlere geländegängige Personenkraftwagen, for light or medium cross-country automobile) with high mobility off-road it was common practice to deliver commercial passenger cars (le, m PwK (o)) with reduced off-road mobility instead. This also applied to light and medium trucks.

In order to improve the situation, by 1940 the Schell-Plan came into effect. The variety of passenger cars was reduced from 52 to 30 and the variety of trucks from 114 to 19. Although the Schell-Plan was an effective catalogue of measures, it was not always possible to distribute enough all-terrain vehicles.

As the war widened and casualties increased, the situation was to deteriorate further.

NOVEMBER 1941

Subordination Chart 1 - 18 Nov 1941
HG Mitte, AOK 4, Panzergruppe 4, IX. AK
StuGAbt 203 attached to 78. and 87. InfDiv

With the onset of winter in November 1941, the assault guns were camouflaged using whatever means available. This soldier uses birch twigs to apply slurry chalk. This assault gun can be easily identified as a vehicle of StuGAbt 203 – the improvised light cover is unmistakable.

On around 3 November the Russian winter began. The German troops on the Eastern Front were literally caught cold. Hitler´s original planning aimed to end the campaign long before the onset of winter. Delays occurred because Soviet resistance was stiffer than expected which was possible because of the country's vast human and materiel resources. The underdeveloped road network was a further hindrance. During the heavy summer rains and the following muddy period even tracked vehicles could not move. Consequenty, the supply chain from the train stations to the fighting troops collapsed.

The battalion's struggle was made more difficult by the harsh onset of winter. Although the frozen ground was passable again within certain limits, the machines failed regularly. Here an SdKfz 9 tows a row of trucks over the icy Rollbahn (advance road).

Vyazma was reached in late October. One of the captured Russian trucks, a GAZ AAA, can be seen in the background.

There is heavy traffic on the main road through Vyazma. At this time, the new light off-road passenger car (VW Type 82), better known as the Kübelwagen, was issued to the troops in increasing numbers. This vehicle belonged to the 5. PzDiv.

This assault gun slid down the embankment and was unable to get back onto the road. The 40 cm tracks could not find a foothold on the slippery ground. Proper winter tracks were not to be introduced until autumn 1942; the available ice cleats were not used. Now another assault gun has to help.

In 1941 the winter came exceptionally early and hard. By early November the temperatures in the Moscow region dropped to – 20° C. In statistically normal years the values are around +1 to – 3° C with lower temperatures occuring only by late December.

The German war machinery in the east was not provided with adequate winter resources. The ordinary soldier had no warm clothing. To make matters worse, the depots in the hinterland could hardly help. Low temperature engine oil, grease and fuel were not available. Weapons were no longer functioning; motor vehicles could not be started.

It is difficult to determine why the Reich did not make adequate provisions in time. The meteorological services monitored the situation but apparently the leadership was unwilling to accept any advice. Already, by August 1941, the 4. Panzerarmee's supply service had given the following more or less helpful advice:

Winter clothing has to be requested through the official channels…

Hitler's stubborn adherence to his plans, certainly caused by his hubris, had impeded any forward-looking planning for a possible winter war. However, the realities would soon force the German leadership had to admit the "end of the summer offensive". By 9 December 1941, the New York Times published a short memorandum:

Nazis give up idea of Moscow in 1941. Winter forces abandonment of big drives in north till spring, Berlin says…

Back to StuGAbt 203. By 10 November Major Krokisius submitted a short situation judgement to the superior Armeekorps summarizing the unit's condition:

Since 2 October the Abteilung was in continuous commitment. From 2 to 17 October "203" attacked alongside the motorway Roslavl - Moscow, then turned to Vyazma. After the battle at Vyasma the further advance to Mozhaysk took place using totally sodden roads. The strain of the last two weeks substantially affected the physical performance of our men. Goodwill and great willing are still prevalent, but such performance cannot be boundlessly called up. Without the steady, indefatigable and exemplary commitment of officers and NCOs the recent combat successes would not have been possible. The high losses among the

officers and NCOs testify this fact.

In detail the troop's performance is impaired by:

– Heavy casualties and the associated psychological distress.
– Deterioration of the physical performance by overexertion, the poor weather, inadequate clothing and insufficient supply.
– Diseases, above all colds, then infestation by lice and scabies.
– The constricted and primitive accommodation during the short phases of rest made personal hygiene and the washing of underwear impossible.
– The long absence of field post also proved negative.
– The state of the soft-skinned vehicles is disastrous. The lack of new allocations and the insufficient supply with spare parts impair combat readiness.

By 13 November 1941, the IX. Armeekorps' organizational structure showed three infantry divisions (78., 87. and 252. InfDiv) under its command. Each division was attached with one battery of StuGAbt 203.

Subordination Chart 13 Nov 1941,
HG Mitte, AOK 4, Panzergruppe 4, IX. AK
Staff and 1./StuGAbt 203 attached to 78. InfDiv
2./StuGAbt 203 attached to 252. InfDiv (5 guns)
3./StuGAbt 203 attached to 87. InfDiv

Again the Abteilung was given some time to maintain and repair its materiel. According to Gassauer's report, the three combat batteries were reorganized during a short pause in Rusa. The first platoon of 3./203 was transferred to 2./203 and 1./203 received a single new assault gun.

For the coming offensive operations the commitment of the Sturmgeschütze was imperative. According their tactical guidelines, the batteries should pave the way for the infantry. Although the five available assault guns were to be split up over the infantry regiments, orders were given to use firm roads only. Since great numbers of T-34s were expected, the assault guns were important assets. However, the divisional com-

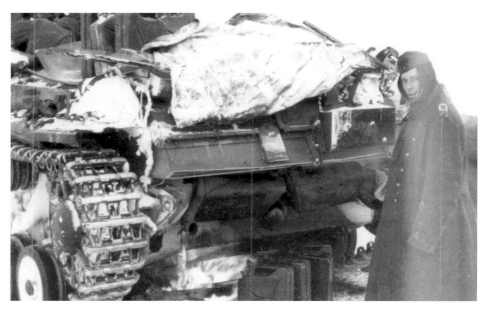

To preheat the engine, an open fire was lit under the hull of this assault gun. Petrol canisters are also heated – a dangerous business. The dark elephant on the secondary candle dropper indicates the 2. or 3. battery.

This photo was taken near Svenigorod, shortly before Moscow. According to the photo's caption, a lowest temperature of - 45° C was reached here. Men and material suffered extraordinarily. This assault gun has not yet been whitewashed, so the markings of the 1. Bttr remain visible.

Despite the snow, the score of this assault gun is recognisable. 13 tank kills were noted on the gun's mantle plate. One aircraft was also destroyed, perhaps on the ground. The 50 mm thick armour shows traces of shelling, presumably either by 45 mm tank guns or PaK.

mander expected self-confidence from his infantry and urged his men to make best use of the 3.7 cm Paks from concealed positions – a pious hope when facing the far superior Russian tanks.

By 16 November the commander of the 252. InfDiv gave the following command to 1./203:

1./StuGAbt 203, Batteriechef Lt Dostler

Enemy broke through own lines at Wajushino (11 km southwest of the lake). Division will launch counterattack in the morning hours of 17. Nov. Assistance of the StuGBttr is requested. The battery will report on 17 Nov at 7.00 am at the command post of InfReg 461. The division must be informed by dispatch rider whether Lt. Dostler decides if a commitment is possible or not."

This rare notice is an example that the evaluation of the tactical situation was left to a Sturmartillerie officer, in this case Lt Dostler. Being the specialist he decided whether his unit could perform the given task and he apparently had the freedom to reject such requests. Indeed the counterattack took place the next day, supported by the Sturmgeschütze. As for the outcome of this action nothing is known.

The war diary of the 252. InfDiv includes a dramatic after-action report written by Lt Seidel, commander of 3./203, dated 26 November:

During the afternoon a 32 t tank tried to attack our lines. It fired a few rounds at a range of 200 m and approached rapidly. Ten rounds fired by our assault guns (HE with impact fuse) had no

252. Inf.-Division.   Div.-Gef.-Std., 16. 11. 1941.
Abt. Ia.   18,3o Uhr.

        An

            1./Sturm-Geschütz-Abt. 2o3,
            Bttr.-Chef Lt. Dostler.

        Russeneinbruch bei Wajuchino (11 km südwestlich
westrand See)!
        Gegenangriff durch Teile der Div. 17.11. vormittags.
        Unterstützung der Sturm-Geschütz-Bttr. hierfür er-
beten.
        Meldung 17.11., 7,oo Uhr Rgts.-Gef.-Std. 461 Wischenki.
        Antwort, inwieweit Beteiligung möglich an Melder der
Division.
                        Für das Divisionskommando
                        Der erste Generalstabsoffizier

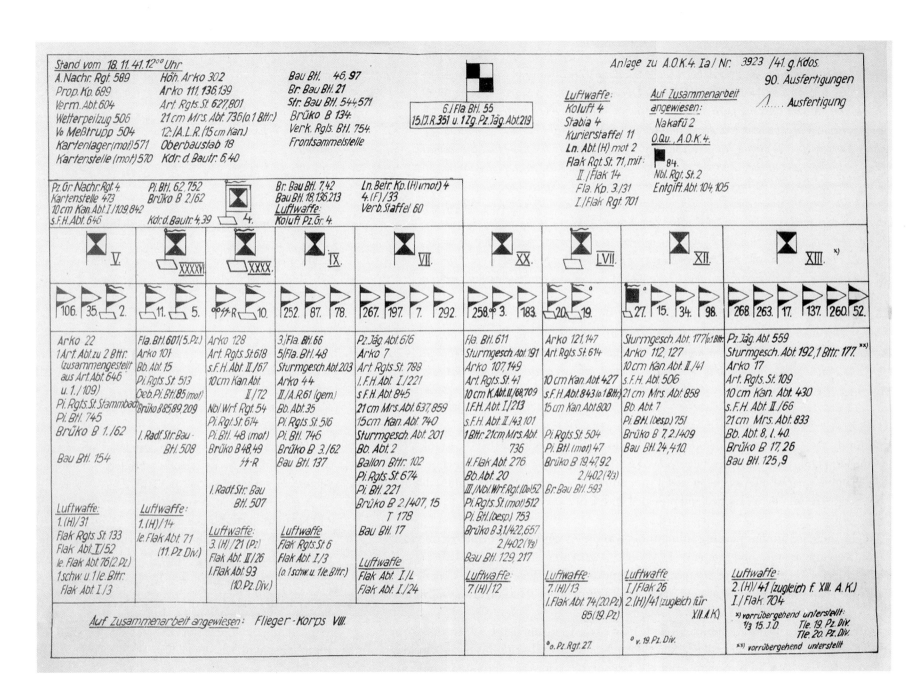

Organisation of the German 4. Armee on 18.11.1941

effect at all. The tank passed left of our assault guns, rolling over a 3.7 cm Pak, whose fire also had no effect. Then the tank crossed a ravine, where our infantry lay in position, entering a 60 by 80 m wide field delimited by a row of trees. ObWm (Oberwachtmeister, a Sturmartillerie NCO rank) Thiemann pursued the tank with StuG no. 33 while I tried to block his way with no. 32. Despite my vehement fire the tank rolled over some strong trees and pushed aside an ammunition truck of the Panzerjäger. The truck fell over, caught fire and exploded. The noise and fire seemed to confuse the commander of the 32 t tank, which now tried to leave the field. Now gun no. 33 blocked the way and sent a barrage of rounds. In the meantime I managed to follow the tank and opened fire from the other direction. This firefight took place at ranges of 20 – 50 m. The numerous grenades hitting tracks, suspension, hull and turret inflicted heavy external damages. Despite this the tank moved in a zigzag manner between the Sturmgeschütze trying to escape. When no. 32's gun got jammed I had to retreat because the Russian approached in order to ram my tank. So I gave way and evaded the enemy. Gun no. 33 turned and sent some rounds behind the accelerating tank.

In all some 70 rounds hit the 32 t tank, the majority at distances of only 20 – 50 m. No hit showed any clear effect. When one round hit the hull's rear, fire flared at the right exhaust for a minute, followed by a trail of smoke. Because of his erratic movement we had the impression that our fire made the tank (commander) feel uncomfortable and confused.

This rather stunning after-action report demonstrates the absolute superiority of the "32 t tank", the Russian T-34 medium tank. Two Sturmgeschütze proved unable to damage a single T-34 at close range. One can easily imagine what would have happened if the commander had not felt "uncomfortable and confused", but had been been better trained and provided with a full ammunition load.

By end of 1941 the standard armour piercing ammunition was the 7.5 cm PzGrPatr, also referred to as 7.5 cm KGr rot (Kopfgranate rot, solid shot red). This APCBC (armour piercing capped, ballistic cap) shell had a penetration of 41 mm at 100 m distance, and 34 mm at 1000 m. Due to its low V° of 385 m/sec the round slipped easily off the slanted armour of the T-34. Furthermore, its accuracy was rather low.

The 7.5 cm GrPatr was the standard HE round normally used against soft and half-hard targets such as dug-in gun positions. According to other publications this round also proved quite effective in blocking or lifting-off the turrets of both T-34 medium and KV heavy tanks. However, the author could not find any such after-action reports.

The concluding words of an officer of the 252. InfDiv seem rather sarcastic:

Seidel's report shows that it is at least possible to repel a 32 t tank by brisk tackling. All involved men deserve full recognition!

Introduction of improved ammunition

Induced by the experience that no German tank weapon was able to effectively combat the new Soviet T-34 medium or KV heavy tank, by autumn 1941 the development of appropriate countermeasures were started. In the long term these works would lead to the introduction of superior tank designs such as the Tiger and Panther tanks. In the medium term the Sturmgeschütze and the coming main combat tank, the PzKpfw IV, would receive a long-barrelled high velocity 7.5 cm gun.

However, the fighting troops needed a quicker solution and German industry decided to develop ammunition able to defeat the threat.

Due to its low calibre length the L/24 gun could achieve only a relatively slow initial velocity dependent on the ammunition used. The HE round (7.5 cm GrPatr 34) could not penetrate any part of the enemy tank's armour. Damages leading to neutralization were possible at very short ranges and by chance only. The AP round (7.5 cm KGr rot) had only poor penetration capability. Furthermore the round slipped off the sloped armour easily. All this led to a considerable waste of ammunition.

One way out was the adaption of a new technology already at hand, the Hohlladungs or Munroe effect. Hollow charges used a conical shaped deep drawn steel sheet. This directed and concentrated the explosive charge in such a way that a jet of plasma and steel particles penetrated even strong armour plates.

By December 1941 the 7.5 cm GrPatr 38 Hl was available for both the StuG and PzKpfw IV. The new round could penetrate 70 mm, theoretically at all ranges.

By February 1942 a new version with an improved shape of cone and increased amount of Hexogen was developed. According to an OKH document armour penetration was 75 mm at 60° impact angle and 45 mm at 45°. The new round was called 7.5 cm GrPatr 38 Hl/B, the older version consequently was given the suffix /A.

Facing limited resources the increased need for Hexogen for the Hl/B was problematic. Exact information on the ammunition's availability is not available.

By 18 November a further assault gun was neutralized by a mine. The 23 November marks a black day; the Abteilung lost six men during a Katyusha raid and a further three were injured.

The extreme cold impaired the combat readiness of the Abteilung. All vehicles suffered from clutch and piston rod damage caused by the low temperatures. Steering linkages and brake systems failed. At temperatures below – 30° C the personnel losses caused by the cold exceeded those caused by enemy fire.

By 17 November the commander of the 252. InfDiv gave orders for his division's further attack on the Soviet capital. 1./StuGAbt 203 under Lt Dostler with five intact assault guns was split – three guns were deployed to InfRgt 461 and two to InfRgt 472.

By 28 November the Ic of the 252. ID (the Ic was the staff officer responsible for enemy reconnaissance and intelligence) reported from the fighting at the 3rd Moscow

defence line. He mentioned the new Siberian troops, which reached the front in the last days of October, emphasizing their good winter equipment, which was in fact far superior to their own. However, the unknown Oberleutnant judged the combat value of the new troops as being rather low. With the help of only two Sturmgeschütze of 3./203, the 252. InfDiv succeeded in breaking though the defence line, taking several hundred POWs and destroying 23 tanks, among them British Mk II Matildas which were encountered for the first time at the Moscow front.

Again the bitter cold, - 41° C, impaired both men and materiel. To start the engines, open fires had to be lid under the few remaining assault guns. In a summarizing after-action report on the problems of winter warfare, the 252. InfDiv noted:

Rusa was reached in November 1941. The town on the river of the same name, Rusa, is located just under 40 km west of Moscow. Two packed assault guns drive into readiness positions. The truck belonged to another unit.

In November 1941, parts of PzRgt 25 of the 7. PzDiv were met. Behind the well-camouflaged assault gun a großer PzBefWg command tank and a PzKpfw 38 (t) are visible.

At snow depths of more than 40 cm, all our tanks quickly became immobile by getting bogged down in ditches or recesses filled with snow. Frozen snow and glaze have the same results. When bogged down, tanks cannot be recovered. Therefore our tanks are bound to roads. In contrast, the Russian T-34 remains mobile. The enemy's anti-tank defence has an easy task. During assault missions, our tanks are bound to the few roads. Forced to move in a line, the rear tank will be destroyed first, blocking the return of the others. The armour protection of our tanks is too weak… For future assault operations we demand delivery of heavy tanks with enhanced off-road mobility.

Again this report by an infantry division does not emphasize the commitment of the attached Sturmgeschütz battalions, in this case "203". This fact is hard to understand. It is, however, possible that the word "tank" in this short excerpt shown above was synonymous with assault gun. However, in the above mentioned situation any commitment of Sturmgeschütze was severely restricted. While tanks with their rotating turret can fire in all directions, Sturmgeschütze with their fixed gun were limited to the driving direction.

DECEMBER 1941

At the beginning of December the remaining combat elements of StuGAbt 203 reached positions some 50 km from Moscow.

Subordination Chart 25 Nov – 29 Dec 1941
HG Mitte, AOK 4, Panzergruppe 4, IX. AK
3./StuGAbt 203 attached to 252. InfDiv

By 4 December 1941 the 252. InfDiv's daily report shows a short entry. The following excerpts are examples:

Own situation:
Today, the 252. InfDiv performed the first retreat operation since the beginning of the war. We retreat with the knowledge that we have been repelled by an enemy far superior in number. During the past weeks we came to realize that the unit was not prepared for the hardship of the Russian winter. Neither garments nor accommodation were appropriate to the specific conditions. Our own anti-tank defence was absolutely incapable; furthermore our troops were not prepared for the impact of the Russian rocket launchers…

Losses at 3 December:
Lost in action:
5 officers, among them one Btl Commander, 50 NCO's and enlisted men.
Wounded:
250 including 30 frostbite cases…

Enemy situation:
Unchanged serious. We have to reckon with further assaults in the course of the night and the following day. Situation of the division remains tense….

Beginning with 5 December 1941, the Soviets launched a counteroffensive against the weakened German formations. The 87. InfDiv was also forced to retreat. A number of disabled assault guns of "203" had to be towed back; one had to be blown up. The transport

This assault gun was also a victim of mines. Russian sappers laid mines in groups, often burying captured German artillery shells. A detonation shredded the running gear and could push up the hull bottom. A quick repair was usually not possible.

of the many POWs caused problems; they followed the Sturmgeschütze on the congested roads. The few remaining Sturmgeschütze were permanently in combat.

Gassauer's recollections report that, by 15 December, mounted enemy forces attacked retreating supply units at Iglovo, near Swenigorod. The helpless casualties in the medical services were all killed.

When subordinated units were dismissed from their commitment it was good custom to end the cooperation with a farewell letter. When 3./StugAbt 203 left its subordination to the 252. InfDiv at the end of 1941, by 29 December 1941 the commanding officer, GenLt Diether von Boehm-Bezing, found words of appreciation:

   To the commander of StuGAbt 203, Major Krokisius

Dear Mr Krokisius!

During the division's hard fighting from 17 Nov to 22 Dec 1941 the 1. Batterie of Sturmgeschütz-Abteilung 203 demonstrated outstanding brotherhood in arms. The unit's men fought briskly in assaults and tough in the defence. Led by battery commander Lt Dostler and battery officer Lt Metzger, 3./203 proved its great abilities and absolute willingness. More than once our struggling infantry were effectively backed by Dostler's battery, a constant source of power for our men.

We sadly accept that the battery will be now needed at other places. I beg you, Maj Krokisius, to submit to your men my own and my men's gratitude.

I wish you and your proud Abteilung all the best and soldier's luck.

Heil Hitler

Signed Boehm-Bezing, Generalleutnant

Even if this eulogy sounds pompous, it proves the high degree of reputation the assault artillery units enjoyed. It should, however, not be forgotten that although the third battery's nominal prowess was six assault guns, only two or three were intact and combat ready by late 1941.

> **Subordination Chart 31. Dec 1941**
> HG Mitte, AOK 4, Panzergruppe 4, IX. AK
> StuGAbt 203 directly subordinated under IX. AK

In February 1942, StuGAbt 203 also had to withdraw to Vyazma. Assault gun "32" of the 1. Bttr seems to be still in good condition. Apart from the frozen snow, no winter camouflage is visible.

One of the three (or four) Truppenluftschutz-Wagen anti-aircraft vehicles, or Kfz 4, of the Sturmgeschütz-Abteilung 203. To brave the low temperatures, the off-road vehicle was equipped with an insulating radiator mask.

In February 1942, the Abteilung was ordered to Kostryza, where the unit´s refurbishment was to take place. Here, Private Kurt Dyck was awarded the Sturmabzeichen.

The Abteilung's doctors, Dr Altvater and Dr Gärtner, took advantage of the time of rest in Kostriza. Altvater wears the normal field uniform, Gärtner the Sonderbekleidung. A reason is not known. In the meantime, Gärtner had also been awarded the Eisernes Kreuz II. Klasse

After this assault gun was overrun by enemy forces during the retreat fighting, the crew had to blow up the vehicle. The detonation tore the vehicle to pieces.

JANUARY TO JUNE 1942

The Soviet counteroffensive was so successful that Heeresgruppe Mitte was forced to retreat to a line some 200 km west of Moscow. The encirclement of the capital had been thwarted.

During the course of January 1942, StuGAbt 203 lay at Pesochnja (Pesochnya) south of Wjasma (Vyasma). The materiel situation was very tense; the number of serviceable assault guns moved towards zero. Since no war diary is available, one has to rely on the reminiscences of the survivors. According to Gassauer, the soldiers were deployed in security missions around the town of Vyasma.

The war diary of the 252. InfDiv reports only two Sturmgeschütze in service with InfRgt 461. Another two in the workshop for repair were notified to be available soon for deployment to InfRgt 472.

By 9 January Major Krokisius was summoned to report to the commanding general of the IX. Armeekorps, GenOb Strauss. Here he was dismissed from his position, initially temporarily. Krokisius was then ordered to organize the establishment of StuGAbt 600.

Command of StuGAbt 203 was handed over to ObLt Behnke on a provisional basis. Behnke had been head of 3. Batterie and his post was assumed by Lt Hagemann.

At that time the Abteilung was unable to fight, having no serviceable Sturmgeschütz. However, the workshop promised to repair four to running condition by 18 January. By 27 January the situation in the area of the IX. AK became difficult. The remnants of StuGAbt 203's three batteries were called back to the staff battery at the Korps level. Of the three surviving Sturmgeschütze, only two reached their mother unit. One had to be blown up.

Three days later a Russian division broke through the German lines at Wjasma. StuG-Abt 203 was ordered to transfer NCOs and enlisted men to reinforce the defence. The overall figure exceeded 50. The assault was repelled and the enemy division smashed.

During February, the OKH gave orders to pull out StuGAbt 203 and 201 (both were attached to PzAOK 4) from active service and to fully replenish them by 25 April (Vollauffrischung).

By 18 February an advance party was established and sent to Kostritsa via Barissau (Baryssau). Here, near the Beresina River, accommodations were prepared for the rest of the Abteilung which arrived by and by, except parts of 1./203. In this phase partisan activity became more and more dangerous. The Heeresgruppe's directives were clear: these deadly attacks should be punished with extreme rigidity. It is not known whether StuGAbt 203 was involved in these measures.

1./203 had to mourn several casualties during their last days of combat. Until the end of March all parts of "203" were reunited at Kostritsa. The men were accommodated by the local population. The coming weeks were spent doing general services such as snow clearing, collection of firewood and the establishment of corduroy roads and spillways.

The 25 April deadline for the replenishment, given by the OKH, could not be met since many of the parts required to carry out the repairs to the vehicles were still missing. By 29 March the new commander, Major Ködel, reached StuGAbt 203. Among his first orders was the preparation of a holiday list, very much to the satisfaction of the men of "203". The Easter days were celebrated with the Ukrainian peasants – apparently relations with them were good.

On 27 April partisans attacked a neighbouring village, killing the village policeman and abducting the mayor. "203" provided their hosts with some hand weapons to defend themselves.

Although by May spring had begun, the weather was still changeable. A part of the Abteilung was on vacation back home while the rest enjoyed generous allocations of provisions.

The materiel replenishment of the Abteilung was carried out in several phases. First, the soft-skinned vehicles were delivered, then the heavier prime movers. The assault guns on the other hand were detained and were to be shipped to the location of the next deployment.

By 24 June, StuGAbt 203 received orders to leave Kostritsa and march in a southeasterly direction.

One of the unit's last assault guns. The gunner observes the terrain; both the scissor telescope and the ZF1 scope are clearly visible.

In the last days before the refreshment, this assault gun received a hit on the superstructure. The gunner was seriously injured by splinters. This and another assault gun were taken along on 22 June 1942, exactly one year after the start of Operation Barbarossa, during the transfer to the southeast.

TO THE CAUCASUS CHAPTER 4

APRIL TO JUNE 42

After the failed offensive on Moscow, Sturmgeschütz-Abteilung 203 was in a poor state in early 1942. Since the stock of operational Sturmgeschütze was low, parts of the unit had to be deployed as infantry. By April, "203" was finally withdrawn from frontline service.

According to a list of Heeresgruppe Mitte dated 9 April 1942, the unit was to be fully refurbished by 25 April 25. The refreshment was to take place in Kostritsa near Barissau (Baryssau). All surviving soft-skinned vehicles were to be left behind. In the small print it was noted that „assault guns still being serviced" were excluded from this. According the sources two StuGs were still available which were to be taken to the new destination. In Kostritsa the unit received soft-skinned vehicles and further materiel. Personnel replacements were also made. Sturmgeschütze were not assigned here, they were to be delivered by rail only upon arrival near the next place of action.

The new equipment also included the famous VW Kübelwagen. The le gl Pkw (passenger car, Kfz 1) was a purposeful development, technically simple and robust. Since the unladen weight was only about 700 kg, the rear-wheel drive vehicle had legendary off-road capability. This vehicle served as a radio vehicle (Kfz 2).

Loading for the new deployment in the southern section. In May 1942 StuGAbt 203 surrendered all vehicles and tractors; only the remaining two assault guns were kept. In Kostriza the unit was equipped with new wheeled vehicles and tractors. The long-barrelled assault guns were to be delivered to the unit only after it reached its destination.

Near Dnjepropetrovsk (today Donetsk), the Dnepr was crossed. Here, three of the new StuG Ausf F "Langrohr" use a pontoon bridge, followed by a Kfz 1 "Kübelwagen". Pioneers instruct the 20-ton vehicles to drive slowly and at intervals.

Again, the trucks were adapted to the necessities. Here the tarpaulin was replaced by a solid wooden body. The exact purpose of this vehicle remains unknown. Often they were assigned to the workshop or the field kitchen. The stacked pneumatic tyres on the driver's cab speak volumes.

On the rails! This photo shows parts of the Transport-Staffel (transport squadron) of StuGAbt 203. A row of Opel Blitz is recognisable. The letter "B" is visible on the flatbed, possibly this truck transports fuel in 20 l canisters. No other insignia are visible.

This photo was taken in Brest-Litovsk in April 1942. The three soldiers, all crew ranks, belonged to a pick-up detachment that was to collect the still missing assault guns. They all wear the allgemeine Sturmabzeichen (general assault badge).

The Abteilung collected the new assault guns in Jüterbog. The Ausf F was equipped with the long-calibre 7.5 cm StuK 40 L/43. This weapon was more than capable of taking on T-34s and KWs even at longer ranges.

The VW Kübelwagen, the Typ 82, was to replace a number of older vehicle types. Technically simple in construction and extraordinarily robust, this vehicle should prove itself very well despite the lack of all-wheel drive. Thanks to the portal axles, the ground clearance was very high.

The new assault guns were delivered in Tropentarnung (tropical camouflage), with sandgrau (sand-grey RAL 7027) patches applied to a gelbbraun (yellow-brown RAL 8020) background at the factory. This camouflage scheme was intended for operations in desert or subtropical areas. The five-digit number is the chassis number.

Sturmgeschütze of Abt 203 on the march south. The tropical camouflage is clearly visible on the front vehicle. No insignia have been applied yet. The barrel is camouflaged by a tarpaulin, an attempt to keep secret the introduction of the long gun.

2./StuGAbt 203

Actual organizational structure 2./StuGAbt 203 as of June 1942 according KStN 446 (Behelf) dated 1 November 1941*
Supply and rear services not shown

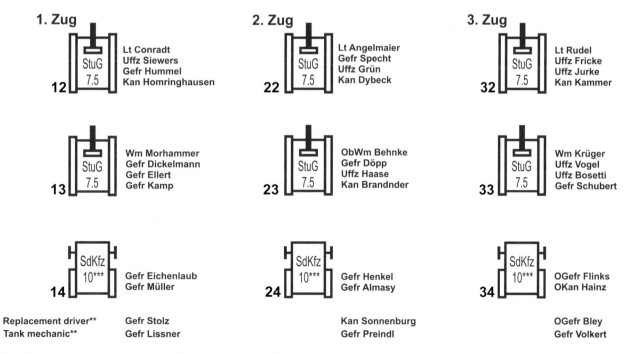

Gruppe Führer

2 StuG 7.5
Olt Dostler
Gefr Burg
Uffz Gaa
Gefr Hengel

Replacement driver** — Gefr Broch
Tank mechanic** — Gefr Lissner

Batterietrupp

Gefr Claus
Gefr Dietrich
Gefr Dick

1 Kfz 2
Okan Ewert
Gefr Broch
Gefr Overmann

Gefechtsbatterie / Geschützstaffel

1. Zug

12 StuG 7.5
Lt Conradt
Uffz Siewers
Gefr Hummel
Kan Homringhausen

13 StuG 7.5
Wm Morhammer
Gefr Dickelmann
Gefr Ellert
Gefr Kamp

14 SdKfz 10***
Gefr Eichenlaub
Gefr Müller

Replacement driver** — Gefr Stolz
Tank mechanic** — Gefr Lissner

2. Zug

22 StuG 7.5
Lt Angelmaier
Gefr Specht
Uffz Grün
Kan Dybeck

23 StuG 7.5
ObWm Behnke
Gefr Döpp
Uffz Haase
Kan Brandnder

24 SdKfz 10***
Gefr Henkel
Gefr Almasy

Kan Sonnenburg
Gefr Preindl

3. Zug

32 StuG 7.5
Lt Rudel
Uffz Fricke
Uffz Jurke
Kan Kammer

33 StuG 7.5
Wm Krüger
Uffz Vogel
Uffz Bosetti
Gefr Schubert

34 SdKfz 10***
OGefr Flinks
OKan Hainz

OGefr Bley
Gefr Volkert

*   Actual structure according to veteran´s records
**   Means of transport not derivable from files
*** Usage of SdKfz 252 or 250/6 amoured ammunition vehicles possible, but not confirmed

On 22 June the remnants of StuGAbt 203 were transferred to Heeresgruppe Süd to take part in Unternehmen Blau where they were attached to the 1. Panzerarmee.

Fall Blau

When the attack on Moscow finally failed in December 1941, the German General Staff was forced to adapt their strategic planning to the changed situation. Hitler, who had proclaimed himself commander-in-chief of the Wehrmacht only recently, now ordered the start of a new major offensive in the southern sector to conquer the important oil fields of Maikop, Grozny and Baku. The background to these plans was the desperate raw materials situation of the German economy. As a desired side effect, the Soviet Union would be cut off from these vital resources, leading to its collapse. The start of this campaign was to be in summer 1942.

In Barissau (Baryssau) StuGAbt 203 was loaded on several trains heading south. The route to the destination Konstantinovka (Kostyantynivka) and Katarinenhof (Katerynivka) went via Roslavl, Kromy, Belgorod, Kharkov, and via Minsk, Assipowitschy, Babruisk, Shlobim, Gomel, Romny, Krementschuk and Dnipropetrowsk.

JULY 42

The units would by and by reach their new accommodations by around 4 July. These villages were old German settlement areas located north of Donets. The men of the Abteilung were apparently welcomed by parts of the population.

Here, 21 "Langrohr-Geschütze", long-barrelled Sturmgeschütze, were taken over. The two surviving Kurzrohr-Geschütze had been taken along during the railway transfer. This would explain the short barrel assault guns that were listed in the few available strength reports until early 1943.

An improved Sturmgeschütz:

One of the pressing issues of the Sturmartillerie (and the Panzertruppe) in 1941 was the 7.5 cm StuG L/24, commonly referred to as "Kurzrohr" (short barrel) ordnance with its insufficient armour penetration force and accuracy. This weapon had been installed in the Sturmgeschütz as a direct support weapon for the infantry. One of the main battle tanks of the Panzertruppe, the PzKpfw IV, was also armed with this weapon. With the increasing importance of being able to effectively engage the superior Russian tanks, the Kurzrohr weapon was of only limited combat value.

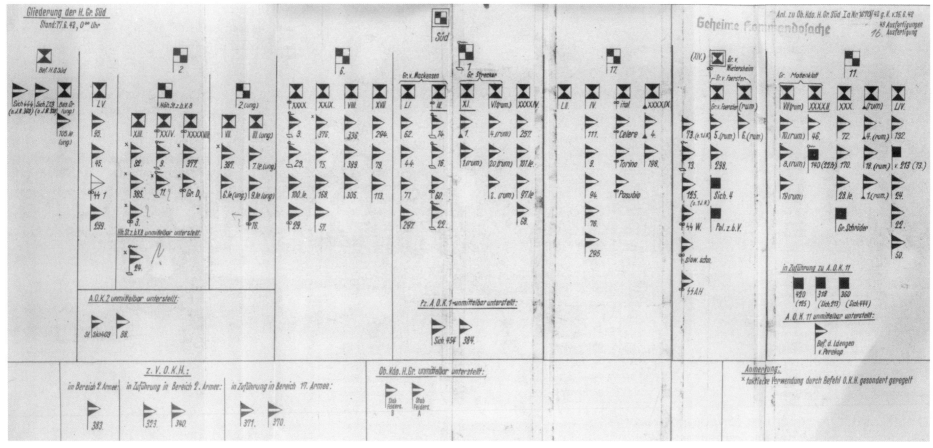

Organisation of the Heeresgruppe Süd on 17.06.1942

The marking of the assault guns of the three combat batteries did not follow a uniform pattern. Here the outline of the elephant was highlighted in red with a stencil. The soldiers are loading 7.5 cm SprGr 34 HE rounds.

This assault gun shows clear, hard-edged camouflage stripes, presumably applied by the crew themselves. Often enough, the units at the front took the liberty of making changes unbureaucratically.

Already by 1940 Krupp and Rheinmetall had been working on a successor for the 5 cm PaK AT gun, which was initially called the 7.5 cm Panzerjägerkanone 44 (later called 7.5 cm PaK 40). The new gun had a calibre length of L/46. Upon availability of this weapon it was quickly adapted for use in tanks or assault guns. Designated as the 7.5 cm StuK 40 (L/43), this gun had a shorter cartridge chamber when compared to the PaK 40. This was necessary due to space limitations in armoured vehicles. A double baffle muzzle brake was added to the gun.

The 7.5 cm StuK 40 fired the following ammunition:

7.5 cm SprGr Patr 34
The standard HE round fitted with impact fuze AZ 23 to be fired with or without delay.

From a hill, this assault gun of the 2./203 takes targets on the other side of the Don under fire. The gunner observes the hits. The antennae of the Ausf F were designed to be folded down. When not in use, they were protected by a wooden trough.

7.5 cm PzGr Patr 39
The standard APCBC (armour-piercing, capped, ballistic cap) shell to combat tanks.

7.5 cm PzGr Patr 40
The PzGr Patr 40 was a Sondermunition (special ammunition) with tungsten core or in British terms APCR (armour-piercing, composite rigid). The low stocks of tungsten led to a very small supply. PzGr 40 projectiles were to be saved for combating heavy tanks only. However, its extraordinary penetrating power only worked at distances of up to about 1000 m.

7.5 cm Gr Patr 38 HL/B, 7.5 cm Gr Patr 38 HL/C
Hohlladungsgeschosse, or shaped charge projectiles (HEAT), were principally an effective and cost-effective technology. Although useful, its accuracy was reduced by their relatively low muzzle velocity and high trajectory. The performance of these shaped charge rounds was gradually improved from version to version.

7.5 cm NbGr Patr
This round was used for smoke firing.

Over the entire war the PzGrPatr 39 was the most numerous and important AT round available for the 7.5 cm StuK 40 L/43. The more powerful PzGr 40 was issued in limited quantity only, as tungsten was a Mangelmaterial (scarce material). The 7.5 cm GrPatr 38 Hl/B (later superceded by /C) was available from September 1942, and was also used in great quantities.

Sturmgeschütz Ausf F
With availability of the 7.5 cm StuK 40 L/43 it was decided to implement the installation of the new gun in the running Sturmgeschütz production as quickly as possible. The design of the Ausf E, whose production had started by September 1941 with an initial order of 500 units, was quickly adapted. However, the superstructure was used with only minor modifications. This resulted in only little resemblance to the Langrohr technology carrier/prototype. It is possible that this was decided in order not to affect the running Sturmgeschütz production. A significantly larger superstructure would be introduced a year later.

The installation of the gun was possible without great changes to the basic design but the larger recuperator system required a greater mantle/housing. On the inside, among other minor changes, new ammunition racks and a roof ventilator for exhausting the irritating powder fumes were installed.

When StuGAbt 203 was newly established, only the new assault guns, that is to say the long-barrelled Sturmgeschütz Ausf F, were issued. Major Ködel supervised the establishment, which took place according to the following organizational structures:

- Stabsbatterie of a StuG-Abteilung according to KStN 416 (dated 1 April.1941)
- Three StuG-Batterien (7 or 10 StuG) according to KStN 446 (dated 1 November.1941)

StuGAbt 203 was authorized to have seven Sturmgeschütze per battery so the unit had a nominal strength of 21 assault guns.

After 120 StuG Ausf F were produced with the L/43, the gun was replaced in production by the 7.5 cm StuK 40 L/48. For unknown reasons, the division received a mixed establishment. This assault gun belonged to the 2./203. A tactical mark was also applied in the battery colour.

Anlage zu Obkdo.d.H.Gr.A, Ia
Nr. 507/42 g.Kdos.v.27.7.42.

Beabsichtigte Verteilung der Heerestruppen im Endziel
auf 11. Armee, 17. Armee, 1. Pz.Armee, 4. Pz.Armee.

	AOK 11	AOK 17	Pz.AOK 1	Pz.AOK 4
Artillerie:				
Art.Kdr.	114,3o6(H) Martinek(H)	14o,132(Geb.) 3o4 (H)	3,6,144/134, 311(H),	1o8,128, 312(H)
Art.Rgt.Stab(mot)	781	617°(Mi), 792°(Mi)	511,7o4	41,7o, 623
Sturm-Gesch.Abt.	"	249	2o3, 21o	191,243
1.F.H.Abt.(besp.)				
1o cm Kan.Abt.(mot)	II./818	634°(Mi)	II./6o,151	43o,II./72, 711
s.F.H.Abt.(mot)	I./77 (t), 737	II./42°(Mi) 844, 154 (t)	6o2,II./52(·) II./65 (o.1)	II./4o I./1o8
s.F.H.Abt.(besp.)				
15 cm Kan.Abt.(mot)	767, 6./A.L.R.2		731	8oo
21 cm Mrs.Abt.(mot. u.beschr.bewegl.)	857		6o7, III./1o9	777 (o.1)
Mrs.Abt.(mot)				
21 cm Kan.Abt.(mot)		732		I./84 (24 cm)
24 cm Haub.Abt.(mot)				
Eisenbahn-Battr.	749°(He)			
schwerste Artillerie				
Beob.Abt.(mot)	43	32, 34	27, 31, 44, 23	28
Ballon-Battr.(mot)				
Wetterpeilzug(mot)	513	514	515	
V°Meßtrupp (mot)	627	512	625	626
Vermessungs-Abt.	617	633	6o2	
Küsten-Artillerie: H.Küsten-Art.Rgt.Stab	938, 766			
H. Küsten-Art.Abt.	774,144,287,7o7, 3./147,284,772, 1./447,3./148, 474,1 Bttr.5o2 (17cm),789°(He), 2./7o7,2./145, 2./147,148,336			

o) He = zugeführt aus Heimatgebiet, Mi = zugeführt aus H.Gr. Mitte

The new underlying organizational structure KStN 446 dated 1 November 1941 principally authorized either seven or ten Sturmgeschütze per battery. It is not known on what basis it was decided whether seven or ten StuG were allocated. The still insufficient production situation may have been one reason.

The intermediate division of the Organisationsabteilung (organization department) of 20 June 1942 shows 19 Sturmgeschütz-Abteilungen, which at the time were all being equipped with 21 assault guns (seven per battery).

StuGAbt 203 retained its two digit vehicle numbering system. A StuG with the number "12" would belong to the first platoon and have the individual number 2. Since a differentiation between the assault guns of the Abteilung's three combat batteries was not possible, the colour system was also retained - white for 1. Bttr, red for 2. Bttr, yellow for 3. Bttr and finally green for Stab and StabsBttr. According to photos, the prominent elephant symbol used on almost every vehicle was painted in one of these colours thus denoting its affiliation to the respective battery.

Back in combat
Immediately after taking over the Langrohr assault guns, training on the new equipment began. Experienced assault gunners, mostly sergeants and non-commissioned officers, waited for the assigned new recruits. Great care was taken to ensure tactical leadership in the battery formation down to platoon level.

Subordination Chart 21 June 1942
HG Süd, PzAOK 1
StuGAbt 203 attached to various divisions

In July 1942 Heeresgruppe Süd was divided into two smaller groups, A and B. StuGAbt 203 was subordinated to A. The next German strategic target was Rostov-on-Don. In anticipation of the attack, the Russian defenders led a counterattack supported by planes on 7 July.

The next day the Abteilung marched towards Artemowsk (Artemivsk). The strong troop movements caused traffic jams on the roads. Among the units involved were mounted Cossacks, who fought on the side of the Germans, mainly in the anti-partisan role.

This photo testifies to the harshness of the fighting. This T-34 Model 1942 was successfully engaged by the assault guns, although no traces of shelling are visible.

During the battles, StuGAbt 203 often worked together with other units. The PzSfl 1, a tank destroyer based on the PzKpfw II Ausf D, carried the Russian 7.62 cm PaK 36 reamed for German ammunition. These vehicles were assigned to the Panzerjäger battalions of various infantry units.

During the transfer march the Abteilung was involved in smaller skirmishes. When parts of the unit drove onto a minefield, the first materiel losses occurred. Several assault guns had to be recovered and repaired and one had to be written off as a total loss. Lt. Rudel was shot in the head and died shortly afterwards in the military hospital.

On reaching Lyssytschansk the River Donez stopped the advance. The Abteilung was forced to halt here for a few days until pioneers built a pontoon bridge.

Stuka dive bombers flew many successful missions beyond the Donez and devastated industrial plants that had already been evacuated. On 13 July the river was crossed and, as they marched on, the Abteilung passed many abandoned freight trains loaded with machinery. The locomotives had been blown up by the fleeing Russians.

One day later the Abteilung was stuck in endless traffic jams again. Fortunately the Luftwaffe had absolute air supremacy here. The Russian artillery also remained quiet; the defenders was too chaotic.

> **Subordination Chart 3 July 1942**
> HG Süd/A, PzAOK 1, III. PzK and XI. AK. StuGAbt 203 attached to various divisions

The advance leads through the immense expanse of the southern Russian Steppe. Huge cornfields were crossed in the summer of 1942. The driver took the photo through his visor.

By 16 July, 1./Sturmgeschütz-Abteilung 203 was attached to the 1. GebDiv which turned southeast covering a distance of over 170 km. The rest of the Abteilung marched on and found shelter in a forest 30 km east of Lissischansk (Lyssychansk).

The vast steppe offered only little cover. The summer weather was treacherous. Heavy rainfall could make the simple roads impassable. The unit´s tracked vehicles were often forced to drag trucks and cars through the mud. Kamensk (Kamensk-Schachtinski) was reached on 21 July, here the Donez was crossed a second time.

By 22 July the three combat batteries moved into their new assembly positions.

Rostov had already been attacked and conquered by German troops in November of the previous year. A Russian counteroffensive liberated the city only a short time later. The intended breakthrough to the Caucasus had been prevented at that time.

The attack on 22 July 1942 hit the Russians in the summer and with much greater force. By this time the German units were equipped with significantly improved weapons; StuGAbt 203 relied on its effective long-barrelled assault guns.

The Abteilung attacked Rostov from the north and the vehicles had to move through the narrow streets of the city. Following street fighting, the assault guns supported the capture of Aksai on the eastern edge of Rostov.

After the end of the fighting in Rostov, Major Ködel gave orders to search the town and confiscate as much ex-Russian materiel as possible. This way some Ford GAZ trucks could be assimilated; a welcome reinforcement of the supply squadrons.

Following this, by July 25 the Abteilung was ordered to the River Don, to the area of Razdorskaya near Schachty. The supply units were located near Novocherkassk, some 10 km to the north. While the pioneers were building a bridge over the great river, the assault guns were forced to wait. Accordingly they were assigned to fight the enemy artillery, dug in on the other bank of the river, in direct fire.

After completion of the bridge on 1 August, the Abteilung could also cross river Don. The last element to follow was the combat train.

AUGUST 1942

The next destination was the Caucasus. Over the next few days the advance went in a south eastern direction through the deserted steppe. Huge fields of grain and sunflowers were passed one after the other. The enemy withdrew into the vastness and did not stand up for battle. The Russians had dispatched most units for the defence of Stalingrad.

This assault gun shows another example of the inconsistent application of markings. The elephant, barely visible, was applied in yellow to the left of the bar cross. The number "33" seems also to be yellow.

3./StuGAbt 203

Actual organizational structure 3./StuGAbt 203 as of August 1942
according KStN 446 (Behelf) dated 1 November 1941*
Supply and rear services not shown

Gruppe Führer

2

Wm Dethloff
Uffz Trabo
Gefr Elbin
Gefr Pühn

Batterietrupp

1 Kfz
Wanderer

Lt Angelmaier**
Uffz Daniel
Gefr Bretsmann
Gefr Debus

Gefr Naumann
Gefr Hühnergart

Gefr Schler
Gefr Schne
Okan Ihse

Gefechtsbatterie / Geschützstaffel

1. Zug

12 StuG 7.5

Lt Angelmaier, Plt leader
Gefr Feyerabend
Gefr Petermeier
Gefr Streit

13 StuG 7.5

Owm Thiemann
Uffz Neusser
Gefr Schattauer
Gefr Hahn

47 Lkw 3 t

***
Uffz Hoffmann
OGefr Adam

2. Zug

22 StuG 7.5

Lt Krämer, Plt leader
Uffz Brechte
Gefr Beckers
Gefr Wagner

23 StuG 7.5

Wm Holluba
Gefr Fischer
Gefr Kreidl
Gefr Bruckmann

48 Lkw 3 t

***
OGefr Titze
Okan Streu

3. Zug

32 StuG 7.5

Olt Kühl
Uffz Völl
Gefr Sch
Uffz Hei

33 StuG 7.5

Wm Gas
Gefr Ne
Gefr Rir
OGefr M

49 Lkw
Beute

***
Uffz Bat
Gefr Rei

---

*   **Actual structure according to veteran´s records**

**   **Lt Angelmaier (battery commander) also assumed command of 1. Plt**

*** **Ammunition trucks from combat train, not reliably documented**

A Kradmelder of StuGAbt 203. The soldier wears the famous Krad coat despite the summer heat. Safety goggles keep out the omnipresent dust. The gas mask container dangles in front of his chest, a report pouch on his belt. Three ammunition pouches indicate his armament, the K 98 carbine.

These unknown soldiers of StuGAbt 203, a non-commissioned officer (OA) and a private, were freshly decorated with the Eisernes Kreuz II. Klasse. The assault gun is well camouflaged in a cornfield, but the tall plants also covered Russian close combatants.

The motor vehicles of the Abteilung had to cover long distances on land marches which meant that the repair units were fully utilised.

By 6 August, the men of the Abteilung saw the Caucasus for the first time. At Armavir the first harsh resistance was met.

Subordination Chart 15 August 1942
HG Süd/A, PzAOK 1
StuGAbt 203 attached to 16. InfDiv (mot) and other divisions

At the beginning of August, this Sturmgeschütz Ausf F (L/43) was destroyed by two hits in the superstructure. The following detonation killed three crew members, the driver escaped slightly injured.

Attached to the 16. InfDiv (mot), the Kuban was crossed by a previously explored ford. Tanks of the 13. PzDiv supported the further attack. With combined forces a bridgehead was built and extended. During the fighting the Chefgeschütz (battery cdr's vehicle) of 2./203 took a direct hit on the roof ventilator. Splinters entered the interior setting the assault gun on fire. OLt Dostler, the commander of 2. Batterie, and two further men fell. The driver survived lightly wounded. The Sturmgeschütz burned out completely and had to be written off.

On 7 August Labinsk, at the foot of the Caucasus, was reached. Here the Abteilung captured a large Russian food depot in an unexpected stroke of luck. The Russian population, Karbadino-Balkarians, turned out to be very friendly and offered their help.

This photo shows the two hits that cleanly penetrated the side armour. The repair company will remove all parts that are still usable and continue to use them.

The 16. InfDiv (mot) now attacked towards Maikop, integrating the assault guns of 2./StuGAbt 203 in the advance party. The advance was disrupted by occasional attacks by Russian biplanes. After two aircraft were shot down, the air attacks subsided. Initially the Abteilung followed other German combat units without a fight and some reports told of large quantities of destroyed Russian war equipment littering the battle route. The huge sunflower fields offered good cover for the assault guns on the one hand, but on the other hand there were scattered Russian soldiers lying in holes in the ground everywhere. Here close cooperation with the infantry was indispensable.

By 10 August, during a short phase of recreation, an unexpected Russian assault took place. Strong forces retreating from Stawropol to the mountains caught the men of 2./203 by surprise. The men were forced to jump into their assault guns in bathing trousers.

From the recollections of an unknown veteran from the Stabsbatterie StuGAbt 203:

Our Geschütz lay in a huge corn field, so it was well camouflaged and hardly recognizable. Around 10.00 o'clock we heard the thunder of guns. Russian artillery covered us with heavy fire. As well as possible we dug holes in the sun-dried black earth and ducked away. In expectation of the enemy breaking through, we grabbed our hand weapons. We already had suffered a number of wounded, some of them badly. Around 11.00 o'clock our assault guns were ready for the counterattack. When they returned in the afternoon, the attack was successfully completed without significant loss. The entire enemy battery was smashed and some American Dodge trucks were captured. Unfortunately, our Lieutenant Conradt was badly wounded, he died in the evening. We all mourned the loss of the sympathetic officer.

After this successful action, the Abteilung-Kommandeur, Major Ködel, and Lt Kojer were awarded the Eisernes Kreuz I. Klasse. Lt Krämer and the medical officer, Dr Altvater, received the Eisernes Kreuz II. Klasse.

Here, the commander, Major Ködel, fell severely ill and had to leave the Abteilung for medical treatment. Hptm Behnke from 3. Bttr took over command, ObLt Angelmaier then assumed the leadership of the battery.

On 16 August, Labinsk was reached and the River Laba was crossed. The next destination was again Armavir, where the Kuban was crossed a second time. Two days later Voroshilovsk (today Stavropol) was reached.

Due to supply difficulties, the unit was taken out of active service and remained in Voroshilovsk for a full month. Since no fuel was available, the leadership of Army Group Don considered deploying the men of the Abteilung in the infantry róle. Hptm Behnke was able to ward off this request in an energetic interview at LVII PzK.

The exploding ammunition also set fire to the fuel tanks. The engine deck was then flung away by the subsequent detonation. The assault gun was certainly a total loss.

SEPTEMBER/OKTOBER 1942

> **Subordination Chart 25. September 1942**
> HG Süd/A, PzAOK 1, LVII. PzK.
> 1./203 attached to 1. GebDiv
> 2./203 attached to 13. PzDiv
> 3./203 attached to 2. Rumanian Mountain Division

In early September, the 2. and 3./StuGAbt 203 were deployed nearer to the Caucasus mountains. The 1. Bttr was directly subordinated to the 1. GebDiv (mountain infantry) and fought successfully near Naltschik (Nalshik) on the Terek. The assault guns were put under heavy strain on the partly steep and winding paths.

The batallion´s medical officer, Dr Altvater, was transferred to a tank regiment in September. He was replaced by Dr Wille and Dr Schwarzfischer.

1./203 still assisted the 1. GebDiv when, on 28. October, heavy Russian counterassaults were repulsed. During a raid on Baksan, the battery lost all Sturmgeschütze due to a well-placed mine field. It is most likely that the assault guns' damaged suspensions could be repaired by the workshop.

On 25 October the decisive attack on Nalchik began; hard fighting took place. From the personal remembrances of F. Gassauer:

> On October 26th the Abteilung advanced to the outskirts of Naltschik (Nalchik). After a counterattack, 2. Batterie together with army FlaK units and infantry were surrounded and had to defend in a hedgehog position. The mission ended at the end of October without any losses but more than 20 T-34s were destroyed.

> On 27. October the attack on Naltschik began with the support of elements of 1. and 2. Batterie. The town was well fortified. At the outskirts well camouflaged concrete bunkers had been established and the windows of the multi-storey houses were converted into loopholes.

> From every house the defensive fire of the Russians whipped towards us keeping down our infantry. After support fire of our Nebelwerfer the assault guns advanced further, closely followed by Romanian and German mountain infantry. Passing by shot-up houses we went on to the centre of the town until we reached a big junction. Here the assault guns turned and rolled along the tracks towards the station. The bunkers built here were shot to pieces in direct fire. The next day Naltschik was firmly in German hands.

While the situation of the 6. Armee in Stalingrad became more and more difficult StuGAbt 203 advanced further to the southeast. This Ausf F (7.5 cm StuK L/43) belonged to the 1. Bttr.

Even in 1942, pure-bred equipment with powerful off-road vehicles was not possible. This commercial passenger car was used by Abteilung´s doctor, Dr. Gärtner. The vehicle, well camouflaged in a field, cannot be identified.

Another shot-up assault gun of the 2. Bttr; the red elephant is clearly visible. The driving visor was blown off, the undercarriage is badly damaged. Nevertheless, a repair was certainly possible. This vehicle carried the longer 7.5 cm StuK L/48 gun.

The supply of important spare parts, and partly also of operating materials, was ensured by air transport. The service life of the Maybach engines was limited, so replacements were vital. Here an HL 120 TRM is being unloaded from a Ju-52.

The Chefgeschütz (bttr cdr´s assault gun) of the 2. battery (red elephant, red no. 1) was hit by several shells at the beginning of August. OLt Dostler fell with two other crew members.

A Maybach HL 120 TRM hangs on the hook of a crane, such as the Kfz 100. Replacing engines was part of the daily work of the maintenance services. If possible, the engines were repaired by the workshop itself. Depending on their condition and mileage, engines were also sent back to the Reich for overhaul.

In October 1942, Nalchik, the capital of the Soviet constituent republic of Karbadino-Balkaria, was reached. The engine covers of the assault guns were packed full, as the crews were forced to stow their belongings outside the vehicles. In the fighting compartment additional ammunition was stacked.

Carelessly camouflaged with corn plants, this Sturmgeschütz Ausf F (L/48) was hauled next to a farmer's cottage. The crew seems to be celebrating the award of an Eisernes Kreuz II. Klasse to an unknown soldier.

The foothills of the Caucasus were traversed on endless serpentine roads. StuGAbt 203 was one of the units that advanced furthest into the southeast of the Soviet Union during Operation Blau.

To cross the countless streams at the foot of the Caucasus, makeshift bridges had to be built again and again. This Sturmgeschütz (L/43, with welded-on 30 mm additional armour) seems to be carefully inching its way on a wooden structure. The soldiers seem to be unsure whether the construction can withstand the 20 t.

NOVEMBER

In November, 2. Bttr was still attached to the 13. Panzer-Division. In his recollections F. Wernz noted increasing problems regarding maintenance and supply of the few Sturmgeschütze. The actual strength is unknown.

During the further advance to Chassanja, the Sturmgeschütze had to overcome steep and rocky mountain passes. According to F. Gassauer's remembrances, many assault guns lost their tracks, neutralizing them temporarily. Because of these delays a Russian general could flee in a plane at the last second.

In these days the fame of StuGAbt 203 increased. Veterans recall that the unit was given nicknames such as Feuerwehr (fire brigade) and Bügeleisen (flat iron). When attached to infantry divisions, which normally had no armoured elements, the combat strength could be considerably increased even by the allotment of only a platoon of two or three StuG to "iron out" any problems.

It was also not unusual that tank divisions were assigned with Sturmgeschütz detachments of Heerestruppen StuG units.

The fighting of the past months claimed many victims from the ranks of StuGAbt 203 and the officer corps mourned the deaths of Lt Döhler (shot in the heart on 5 November) and ObLt Ostertag (hit by a PaK bullet to the chest on 29 November). The battery commander of the 3. Bttr, ObLt Angelmaier, was injured by shrapnel during a tank battle. Finally Lt Krämer was also injured by splinters in Naltschik after an anti-tank rifle hit. When, on 22 November, ObLt Metzger left the Abteilung to assume a training post in Jüterbog, only two officers from the old 1941 officers' corps remained.

By 28 November a new army group, Heeresguppe Don, was installed between Heeresgruppe A and B. StuGAbt 203 was now subordinated to HG Don.

Subordination Chart 29 November 1942
HG Don, PzAOK 4
StuG 203 attached to 6. and 23. PzDiv

StuGAbt 203 apparently still used older vehicles such as this Kfz 1 at the end of 1942, as can be seen here in the foreground. The VW Kübelwagen in the middle was used as a light radio vehicle (Kfz 2). The truck in the background, possibly a Lend-Lease Chevrolet, was captured and put to further use.

Sergeant Lissmann, Lieutenant Ostertag and the Privates Jokisch and Dyck at their assault gun. The muzzle brake of the 7.5 cm StuK 40 L/43 shows a coating to help against fouling. The picture was taken at the Kuban in August 1942.

This car of the 1. Bttr, obviously a Wanderer W 35, was assigned to the repair company. Commercially available vehicles were also partially militarized, and received Notek camouflage headlights.

In the coverless plains of southern Russia, camouflage was essential for survival. Standard vehicles like this Opel Kadett, which had no off-road capability to speak of, were still assigned. A box for 2 cm ammunition served as a "Fresskiste" (food box).

Well camouflaged in a cornfield, a soldier uses the box-like gun mantlet of his assault gun for writing. The clearly visible steel plate is 50 mm thick.

During the fighting on the Kuban, Corporal Jokisch also received the Eisernes Kreuz II. Klasse. The cross hangs on the ribbon and is buttoned into the buttonhole. Note the loop on the epaulette, here the Abteilung's stitched No. 203 is exceptionally clearly visible.

Lieutenant Metzger's batman, an unknown gunner, fetching food. The Sonderbekleidung is visible here in full detail. In addition to the general Sturmabzeichen, the soldier also wears the ribbon of the EK II. Klasse.

In the "Schreibkoffer"(clerk´s writing van). Standing visible is Hauptwachtmeister Beims, the division's sergeant major. The sleeve stripe indicates his official position; that of a sergeant major. The bombarde symbol was the sign of the artillery training regiment in Jüterbog.

Kurt Dyck was a gunner and radio operator of an assault gun. This photo shows him with (besides a very long cigar) headphones and a throat microphone as well as dust goggles. Visible in front of him is the fume ventilator, which was very sensitive to bullets due to its exposed position.

The "writing room" of the staff battery of StuGAbt 203 was housed on an Opel Blitz with a box body. This superstructure had been built by the battalion with its own means. In order to make progress on the slippery ground, snow chains were put on. In the front, the staff battery's Wanderer Pkw (car) is visible, now badly damaged.

In early 1943, StuGAbt 203 received replacements for losses. This assault gun belonged to the Ausf F/8 production, and shows screwed-on 30 mm additional armour at the front. With this, 80 mm of armour protection was achieved. The gun was apparently torn apart by a barrel burst.

The T-34/76 was the most frequent opponent of the assault guns. If this was still almost invincible for the Panzerwaffe in the spring of 1942, the situation was to change after the introduction of the 7.5cm KwK 40/Sturmkanone 40. At first glance, however, this 1942 model appears undamaged.

DECEMBER 1942

Under this subordination, StuAbt 203 mainly assisted the 17. and the 23. Panzerdivision. This was a purely organizational measure; the reinforcements for the hard-fought German units were few in number.

Subordination Chart. December 1942
HG Don, StuGAbt 203 directly attached to PzAOK 4, partly attached to 17. PzDiv

---

By 2 December, Heereszeugamt Magdeburg (army depot) authorized the "anticipated" shipment of 15 Sturmgeschütze (lang) to StuGAbt 203. When available, they were allocated by the Army Group or Army High Command. These replacements were normally based on the requirements of the individual units.

The Red Army also continued to use old materiel for a long time. So it should come as no surprise that the division still encountered T-26 and BT-7 tanks in 1943. Under normal circumstances they were easy to fight with assault guns but, when fired on from the side, the Russian 45 mm cannon could also be dangerous.

From September 1942, the troop received the new Ausf F/8 assault guns. Apart from minor changes, these now had armour reinforcement fitted to the front of the vehicle. 30 mm plates were welded on or, as here, screwed on. The recuperator of this 7.5 cm StuK 40 L/48 seems to be defective; the barrel lies far back in the gun mount.

On this F/8 the screwed-on additional armour can be seen in every detail. This vehicle was also delivered in Tropentarnung, the camouflage spots stand out clearly against the base colour.

This assault gun belonged to the third platoon of 2./StuGAbt 203, the red elephant is quite clearly visible. The number "31" appears to be black. Despite the wintry environment, no wide winter tracks were put on as relatively little snow fell in the southern section.

It is possible that (besides necessary deliveries of replacements) this reinforcement was the result of the decision to boost the battery's strength from seven to ten Sturmgeschütze.

Anyhow, for the Abteilung this was a welcome increase of combat power.

Sturmgeschütz-Abteilung 203 remained in the Caucasus Mountains until mid December. Following new orders the Abteilung then turned north and marched via Ssalsk to Remontnaja (Remontnoye). At around this date the Heeresgruppe decided to stop the advance to the Caucasus. All units were to be transferred to relieve the 6. Armee in Stalingrad.

By 22 December, PzAOK 4 issued the order to attach Sturmgeschütz-Abteilung 203 to the 23. PzDiv. StuGAbt 203 received orders by the Ia officer of the LVII Panzerkorps to move to Kotelnikovo. At that time StuGAbt 288 was also part of the PzDiv which had to supply both units with fuel. A delivery of 100 m³ petrol sent to the 23. PzDiv was soon spent.

At around this date Unternehmen Wintergewitter (Operation Winter Storm), the attempt to relief the enclosed 6. Armee, was cancelled. The situation of the German soldiers and their allies in Stalingrad finally became hopeless.

Two days later "203" was again attached to the 17. PzDiv. The rapidly changing subordinations once again illustrate the dynamics of the fighting. On around 24 December the Abteilung received the following message:

> *To StugAbt 203. Intervene at Generaloff, if necessary block off here. 17. PzDiv will arrive soon. What is the situation there?*

Regarding supply, the Abteilung was dependent on the respective superior unit, in this case the LVII. PzK. Immediately after being attached, the corps' quartermaster officer arranged the delivery of a Verbrauchssatz fuel allowance in Remontnaya. The consumption rates for covering a distance of 100 km were related to the normal equipment of a StuGAbt according to KStN, a quantity of roughly 17,000 l.

By 23 December Lt Gassauer travelled to Dnepropetrovsk to pick up new Maybach HL 120 engines for the Sturmgeschütze. A reliable supply was vital for the Abteilung's operational readiness, so this long journey (some 800 km) was undertaken.

Subordination Chart 22 December 1942
HG Don, StuGAbt 203 directly attached to PzAOK 4

Christmas was celebrated in positions around Kotelnikovo.

In the cold of the Russian winter, the fighting compartment of this assault gun was warmed up by an external heater for repair works. Note the two foldable aerials.

Kurt Dyck has meanwhile been promoted to Wachtmeister (sergeant). The battalion number "203" is visibly embroidered on his epaulette.

After the disastrous experiences of the first winter of the war, the equipment of the German units was significantly improved at the end of 1942. This crew wears the padded reversible uniforms that reliably protected them from the cold. The soldier on the left also has mittens. A jester has put on a captured Russian officer's uniform.

During 1942, Allied aid deliveries to the Soviet Union reached a first peak. Among other things, the USA supplied M3 Light Tanks, highly mobile vehicles. This was apparently captured undamaged by StuGAbt 203.

This Sturmgeschütz Ausf F/8 was supplied in the field during the operation near Kotelnikowo on 25 December 1942. The vehicle stands uncamouflaged on the uncovered steppe. In the background is an Opel Blitz with a box body, possibly with a technical defect.

In the southern section of the Eastern Front, the Russians still used a large amount of old equipment. This T-26 became an easy victim for the assault guns, the 7.5 cm PzGrPatr 39 presumably completely penetrated its 16 mm armoured turret.

In a rare period of calm, these assault guns (presumably of the 1. Bttr) cross a shallow stream. The superstructure is covered by the large vehicle tarpaulin to protect against rain. Large amounts of luggage are stowed on the engine deck, including a 200 l fuel drum.

STURMGESCHÜTZ-ABTEILUNG 203 RELIEVING THE 6. ARMEE

CHAPTER 5

In the spring of 1943, the division repeatedly had to detach men to secure the lines of retreat. These soldiers are equipped with MP 40, submachine guns (9 mm calibre) for close combat.

To lift the bad mood, the commander had alcohol allocated. While waiting at Isjum, the young soldiers were housed in solid, good accommodation.

By the end of 1942 the situation of the German 6. Armee became critical. Already by late summer of 1942 more than 300,000 men had been cut off and encircled in Stalingrad. Although the situation was hopeless, Hitler insisted on holding the city. A breakout to the German lines would have been possible but all respective wishes were bluntly rejected.

The supply situation became increasingly tense despite an air bridge being established. At the end of January 1943, most soldiers stopped fighting, partly on orders by their immediate superiors, partly due to lack of materiel and food.

While the men of StuGAbt 203 were still hoping to be able to celebrate a quiet Christmas in their new, simple accommodation near Kotelnikovo, orders were issued on December 24 to attack the Russian containment ring around Stalingrad from the south. During the next 14 days the men of the division fought in icy cold conditions against a stubborn enemy.

A success report for this period recorded the destruction of:
- 44 medium T-34 and heavy KV tanks
- 9 light tanks
- 14 artillery guns
- 11 heavy AT guns
- 46 light AT guns
- 25 vehicles

The Abteilung also had heavy losses. OLt Angelmaier, who had left the sickbay only recently, received a bullet in his neck on 11 January. Lt Gassauer was wounded by mine splinters.

Now Lt Koch became Batterieführer (battery commander) of 3./203. He would lead the battery only for a few days; he died by 14 January due to a headshot.
At that time the LVII. PzK considered amalgamating the remnants of StuGAbt 203 and 243. Although these plans were discussed and some preparations were done, these plans were finally cancelled.

By 5 January, 3./203 submitted an after-action report:

Unit advances to the height 59.2, launching a counterattack against Wishnjakov. 3./203 fought against infantry, AT guns and machine guns only. We destroyed two AT guns and four heavy MGs. Following this the unit gave fire support for establishing a bridgehead north of Sserebrjakovka and fought against infantry and tanks, destroying four tanks without own losses.

The unit fired 22 PzGrPatr 39 (AP), ten SprGrPatr 34 (HE) and 108 PzGrPatr 38 (Hl).

Signed: Lt Koch

The expenditure of ammunition is interesting. While combating enemy tanks normally the PzGr 39 was preferred. 3/203 almost exclusively used hollow charge projectiles. A possible explanation would be a bottleneck in the supply of the standard PzGr 39 APCBC round.

The soldiers of the StuG battalions took on the infantry tasks reluctantly, lacking both suitable weapons and the necessary training.

Snow could fall until April. These two Ausf F/8 assault guns were waiting for a Russian attack across the Donets. The Abteilung was constantly in action to prevent the establishment of permanent bridgeheads

By 9 January both Sturmgeschütz-Abteilungen reported that 7.5 cm ammunition was running short. This problem applied to all units involved in the fighting, which further worsened the situation. For instance, for a Tiger-Abteilung on site (either 2./s PzAbt 502 or s PzAbt 503), a "Laboriermaschine" (final assembling machine for ammunition) was flown in by Ju-52 transport so that 8.8 cm FlaK ammunition could be converted and fired.

Supply problems were omnipresent. By 7 February the Abteilung reported seven immobilized Sturmgeschütze and demanded the delivery of a s ZgKw 18 t (SdKfz 9) heavy tractor to recover the precious and otherwise undamaged materiel. PzAOK 4 had to reject this demand after explaining the difficult situation. The tank army had

the task of recovering more than 50 tanks with only six intact ZgKw (tractors). The commander of StuGAbt 203 declared that without help from another unit he would find himself constrained to blow up all seven assault guns. The further fate of these Sturmgeschütze is not known.

Sturmgeschütz-Abteilung 203 now retreated with the 17. PzDiv via Salsk to Rostov. The war diary of LVII. PzK noted that the Russians heavily attacked the positions of both the 17. and 23. PzDiv. Now the fuel supply situation also became critical; a train could not get through because the line was blocked by an ammunition delivery for the SS Wiking Division.

By 10 January, the LVII. PzK applied for aerial transport of ammunition for StuGAbt 203. On the same day the unit was instructed to reconnoiter a landing place for a Ju 52 transport plane. In this situation, StuGAbt 203 was alternately attached to the 17. and 23. PzDiv. On 21 January the unit finally received 500 rounds of 7.5 cm ammunition.

The third battery's commander, Lt Koch, fell on 14 January by an infantry bullet. During the retreat, fighting in association with the 17. PzDiv, he had destroyed six tanks, 11 AT guns, and three 7.62 cm field guns. Koch was awarded the Eisernes Kreuz II. Klasse posthumously.

Under the pressure of the attacking Russian units, Heeresgruppe Don had been pushed back to the lower reaches of the Don. In this situation the German units were regrouped. Specifically, on 23 January 1943, a new army was formed from the General Command of the XVII. Armeekorps. Armee-Abteilung Hollidt, named after and commanded by General Karl-Adolf Hollidt, was subordinated to Heeresgruppe Don and Heeresgruppe Süd. The formation was only to exist for a short time; on 6 March Armee-Abteilung Hollidt was redesignated as the 6. Armee.

Towards the end of January it became clear that all German attempts to rescue the 6. Armee were in vain. On 25 January the Soviets succeeded in splitting the enclosed German units into a south and a north cauldron. Only three days later the northern cauldron was split again into a central and a northern section. By 31 January the Soviets succeeded in taking the 6. Armee headquarters and the struggle for Stalingrad was over.

By 27 January Major Ködel returned to the Abteilung and took the lead again. Hptm Behnke was ordered to Jüterbog, where he took command of a new Sturmgeschütz-Abteilung.

By mobilizing all forces, the Soviets now succeeded in regrouping parts of their units and diverting them to the west. Now the German units south of Stalingrad were also endangered. Heeresgruppe Süd now ordered the evacuation and retreat in order to escape the confinement.

This Sturmgeschütz Ausf F/8 shows the wide winter tracks that became available in autumn 1942. With the ground pressure reduced by almost 1/3, the mobility in snow and slush was clearly better.

The Sturmhaubitze - meeting artilleristic needs again

The Sturmgeschütz 7.5 cm L/24 had proven its value during the French campaign and the early stage of the invasion of the Soviet Union. It fulfilled its tactical mission of assisting the infantry in the front lines with effective support fire down to the ground. The high ammunition storage of up to 100 rounds (and more unofficially stored) allowed long and efficient missions. Originally the L/24 armed assault guns would combat tanks only in an emergency or in self defence. This would change by 1941. While the light Russian tanks encountered at the beginning of the Ostfeldzug were no match for the Sturmgeschütze, the modern T-34 medium and heavy KV tanks that were unexpectedly encountered would change the situation absolutely. Even with a great expense of ammunition, the Sturmgeschütz "kurz" (short-barrrelled) turned out to be clearly inferior. As already explained, this unfavorable situation led to the development of the long-barrelled 7.5 cm StuK 40.

Already by October 1940, the General der Artillerie (with the experiences of the commitment in France at hand) had established a commission with the task to investigate the future establishment of the artillery. As for the Sturmartillerie, the commission came to the following conclusions:

Assessment:
The fundamental idea of the Sturmgeschütz proved sound, as the first experiences of the frontline batteries showed… Regarding the ordnance, it must be pointed out that a longer gun having a higher V° would result in a flat trajectory. Thus firing over the heads of friendly infantry will be impossible and an enemy in troughs or lightly fortified covers couldn't be combated… According to orders of the honorable commander-in-chief of the army, the Sturmgeschütz shall assist the infantry while penetrating the enemy's zone of resistance in cases where our own artillery can't work. As a result, the Geschütz has to be small and agile above all, in order to reach any objective and to be inconspicuous. Heavier vehicles or longer guns would hinder…

This interesting comment shows that there were different views within the inspectorate of the artillery. Although the commission had broadened the limits of the Sturmartillerie's deployment by introducing new requirements, the assessment in this report sounds like a rebuke, conserving the status quo. However, the report mentions further opinions:

Dissenting opinion of WaPrüf 1 (ammo and ballistics) and WaPrüf 4 (artillery)
It should be proved whether an ordnance of higher calibre able to fire at higher angles should be introduced. A 15 cm weapon, the sIG 33 could be mounted in an armoured tracked vehicle…

This is the first hint of the installation of considerably stronger ordnance in the Sturmgeschütz, or similar infantry support vehicle. The 15 cm sIG 33 was the standard heavy infantry gun in service with infantry and rifle units. Attempts to create a self-propelled version had already been undertaken before the French campaign. The first solution, mounted on the hull of the PzKpfw I, proved to be unsuitable due to the overburdened chassis' low mobility and its high silhouette.

Anyhow, it is quite apparent that parts of the inspectorate of the artillery called for better armament for the Sturmgeschütz. This was rather farsighted, since by September 1940 the long-barrelled Sturmgeschütz with higher V° was far from being at hand. During the year 1942, further development work was undertaken to fill the looming gap in the Sturmgeschütz' application range.

By mid 1942 mass production of the 7.5 cm StuK 40 armed Sturmgeschütz was in full progress. While the available after-action reports drawn up at that time are filled with positive stories praising the StuK 40's vastly improved impact against enemy tanks, no hint could be found of complaints relating to its reduced artillery virtues. However, since at that time most units had still great stocks of L/24 armed Sturmgeschütze at hand, the fighting troops possibly considered this shortcoming not too severe.

In this situation the General der Sturmartillerie demanded the accelerated development and introduction of a heavier calibre gun to assist the 7.5 cm StuK 40 armed Sturmgeschütze. It was decided to pull up the 10.5 cm le FH 18 M for installation in the Sturmgeschütz. Being the standard German light field howitzer, ammunition for this gun was available throughout the front in sufficient quantities. A first Versuchsstück

(test example) was available as early as March 1942 and subsequently a small trial series of 12 units was ordered. Due to manifold problems, nine were delivered by October 1942 and a further three by January 1943. These first vehicles, designated as Sturmhaubitze, were all manufactured using refurbished Sturmgeschütze Ausf E and F sent back from the front. Nine of them were immediately sent to Heeresgruppe Süd, where they were integrated into StuGAbt 185.

The new Sturmhaubitze would enter production by March 1943 but it was based on the new Auf G. The adapted field howitzer received the designation 10.5 cm StuH 42. It could fire the standard ammunition of the 10.5 cm le FH 18. This ammunition was loaded in two parts and, for usage in the Sturmhaubitze, the cartridge was to be fitted with an electric fuze.

The 10.5 cm StuH 42 could fire a range of HE shells with an impact or combination fuse. Smoke shells were also available. Maximum firing range was 10,675 m (6th charge). The 10 cm PzGr rot was the standard armour piercing (APCBC) round. While being in use with the le FH until 1942, it was taken out of service when hollow charge technology became available. Old stocks, however, were used up. The new hollow charge round was called 10.5 cm GrPatr 39 rot Hl/A, B or C. Analogous to the 7.5 cm PzGrPatr 38 Hl, the penetration data reached 75, 80 and 90 mm. For the Sturmhaubitze the 10.5 cm GrPatr 39 rot Hl/A, B or C was delivered cartridged in one piece to increase the rate of fire against tanks.

A new version
By early 1943 a new production version was introduced, the Ausf G. This version showed a redesigned superstructure offering more space. By February a second manufacturer, MIAG, was called upon. Now the production of Sturmgeschütze was ramped up. While during 1942 some 792 vehicles were delivered, this number increased to 3011 during 1943, 3804 during 1944 and a further 863 from January to April 1945 (these numbers included 7.5 cm StuK 40 Sturmgeschütze and 10.5 cm StuH 42).

Organizational issues:

During the year 1942, a new organizational structure was implemented. While initially each Sturmgeschütz-Abteilung was authorized to have 18 assault guns (six in each battery), this number would be increased to 30 (ten per battery). At around end of 1942, the Abteilung-Kommandeur would be issued with a further assault gun. With availability of Sturmhaubitzen it was planned to provide the battalions with two thirds Sturmgeschütze and one third Sturmhaubitzen. This goal was never achieved.

A strength report of StuGAbt 203 dated 1 May 1943 quotes 31 Sturmgeschütze (7.5 cm StuK 40) – no Sturmhaubitzen had been issued so far. In fact the monthly strength reports prove that no Sturmhaubitzen were delivered until re-establishment in the summer of 1944.

FEBRUARY 1943

By 14 February Rostov-on-Don had to be given up. Five days later, by 19 January, orders were given to retreat to the area northwest of the city. Except for StuGAbt 203, more units were involved in the transfer:

- 17. PzDiv
- 23. PzDiv
- SS-Division Wiking
- StuGAbt 243

Subordination Chart

26 February 1943

HG Don, Armee-Abteilung Hollidt, LVII. PzK

StuGAbt 203 attached to 17. PzDiv

By October 1942 the German High Command had ordered the establishment of a static defence line alongside the River Mius, reaching from Taganrog for some 150 km to the north. The Mius-Stellung (Mius Line) consisted of shelters and bunkers, ma-

Wherever possible, fuel reserves were carried; here the soldiers are trying to stow a 200 l barrel on the engine deck. The vehicles were not yet marked with the elephant.

Hauptfeldwebel Beims, the Spieß (company sergeant major) of the 1./StuGAbt 203. The soldier wears the EK I. Klasse as well as the buttonhole ribbons for the EK II. Klasse, and the Eastern Medal. The general assault badge is pinned under the cross. The double laces for his rank as company sergeant major are visible on the sleeves.

In February, sub-zero temperatures were reached again. The soldiers used what was available to them.

chine-gun nests and mobile artillery positions, as well as minefields, trenches, tank obstacles and barbed-wire enclosures. The minefields were at least 200 m deep and secured by 20 to 30 shelters and bunkers per km². Although large parts of the Mius-Stellung were only weak, the Russian offensive was held back until October 1943.

In several marches, mainly carried out at night, the German units retreated westwards. By 17 February the Mius-Line was reached according to plan. In the following days the Soviets broke through at two places and tried to encircle the retreating German

Kradmelder, motorbike dispatch riders, had a thankless job in winter. The heavy motorbikes were difficult to drive in mud and snow, despite the powered sidecar. This photo was taken in February 1943 near Rostov.

Rostov-on-Don had to be abandoned in February 1943. The few operational assault guns of the Abteilung secured the withdrawal of the German troops.

Rostow was very important for the German units. The forest of signs testifies to the large number of units located here.

Caucasus forces. The breakthroughs could be blocked and the the enemy forces were annihilated during the following days.

During this fighting, by 23 February 1943, the commander of StuG 203, Major Ködel, was severely wounded by a tragic accident and died some hours later. Now ObLt Feurstein assumed the responsibility of command.
By 26 February 1942, Armeeabteilung Hollidt submitted a strength report in which StuGAbt 203 reported 27 Sturmgeschütze, of which only eight were fully operational. Ten were in short-term repair and a further eight (plus one short-barrelled version) in long-term repair.

Since the Abteilung was needed more urgently at other focal points, orders were given to transfer to Kharkov in mid-March. When the city was reached, Hptm Behnke arrived unexpectedly. Meanwhile promoted to Major, he was to take over the leadership of StuGAbt 203.

By 9 March, Heeresgruppe Don was renamed HG Süd. At the end of March the high command of Heeresgruppe Süd gave orders for the replenishment of the units under its command. Subsequently four new Sturmgeschütze were authorized for Sturmgeschütz-Abteilung 203. The Abteilung was given a week's rest, which was used to repair damaged materiel and to replenish stocks.

Some days later orders were given to move by rail towards Kharkov. Because of an attack by Polikarkov Po-2 ground-attack planes, called "Nähmaschine" (sewing machines) by the Germans, the first loading had to be stopped. The next attempt took place in deep mud. Because of manifold problems it would last until 17 March when the Abteilung reached Losowa station. Following this, all batteries were transferred to the Isjum area at the River Donez in a land march. Here Major Behnke, who had recently been promoted to Major and awarded the Knights Cross, joined the Abteilung again and took over command. Only a few days later Behnke was severely wounded when three bones in his right hand were destroyed by infantry bullets. He was subsequently transported to a military hospital in Königsberg. By 24 March, Olt Feuerstein assumed command again.

> **Subordination Chart**
> 17 March 1943
> HG Süd, Armee-Abteilung Hollidt, LVII. PzK
> StuGAbt 203 attached to 15. InfDiv

In March 1943, four new assault guns were assigned to the Abteilung (battalion). Despite the icy winter, vehicles with tropical camouflage were again delivered.

Oberleutnant (first lieutenant Angelmaier took command of the 3. Bttr again on 13 December after a stay in hospital. A mere month later, the officer dropped out again after being wounded.

Oberleutnant Angelmaier at his Chefgeschütz. The front armour was now 80 mm thanks to the screwed-on 30 mm plates. This should be sufficient against fire from 7.62 cm weapons until 1943. Combined with the low firing height, assault guns were effective weapons that could prevail even against superior forces.

APRIL 1943

Russian units tried repeatedly to cross the Donez. Thanks to the thin German defence lines they often succeeded in establishing bridgeheads on the river's western banks. The Abteilung rushed from focal point to focal point, fighting these bridgeheads as a "fire brigade". Combat lasted about a week and was to claim many victims on both sides. By 28 April an entire battery, 2./StuGAbt 203, with six StuG was moved into the Tschepel (Chepil) Valley as a mobile operational reserve in case of a Russian attack.

Assault guns were sensitive to lateral fire. Both 45 mm and 76.2mm were easily able to penetrate the 30mm armour plating of the hull and superstructure. The 14.5mm anti-tank rifles (PTRS and PTRD) could also be dangerous at short ranges – this reason enough for the crews to attach additional chain links.

The supply of wide winter tracks was apparently not organised uniformly at all batteries. This assault gun of StuGAbt 203 is waiting to be taken away, the tow rope could indicate damage.

The 4-man crew of a Sturmgeschütz of StuGAbt 203, a non-commissioned officer and three enlisted ranks. The three soldiers on the right wear the buttonhole ribbon for the Ostmedaille on their lapels, the lance corporal on the left also wears the buttonhole ribbon for the EK II. Klasse.

In the first quarter of 1943, the Abteilung's assault guns were deployed in an extensive area. They had to cover great distances in order to be able to intervene in critical situations. The materiel suffered under the strain. The number of operational vehicles fell to four by 29 March 1943.

MAY 1943

Subordination Chart
4 May 1943
HG Süd, PzAOK 1, LVII. PzK
StuGAbt 203 attached to 17. PzDiv and 15. InfDiv

By the beginning of May, PzAOK 1's order of battle for StuGAbt 203 quoted the full target of 31 Sturmgeschütze. However, only 21 were operational. The unit was attached to the 17. PzDiv and the 15. InfDiv of LVII. Panzerkorps. By 25 May the 17. PzDiv was transferred to the XXIV. Panzerkorps.

Realizing this weakening of the German units, a day later the enemy increased reconnaissance activities. The KTB of PzAOK 1 reported:

> In the area of the 15. InfDiv the enemy launched a recon-naissance mission in which one Lt and two men were cap-tured. By 27 May, at 4 am, rocket launchers fired from the direction of Schiritowka to the Tschepel area. Our artillery returned the fire. In the afternoon the positions of the 198. InfDiv were hit by some 200 rounds fired from 7.62 cm guns and heavy grenade launchers. During the night, lively scout-ing party activity was observed; assault squads broke through to Nizhne Russky Bishkin. The attack was repulsed with the help of an assault gun. Casualties: 1 dead, 2 wounded, 12 missing.

Subordination Chart
25 May 1943
HG Süd, PZ AOK 1, LVII. PzK
StuGAbt 203 attached to 15. InfDiv and 198. InfDiv

In May 1943, StuGAbt 203 received for the first time assault guns of the Ausf G. With this new version the superstructure could be enlarged and simplified in shape. The greatest advantage, however, was the rotating commander's cupola, which made it possible to observe the terrain from inside the vehicle.

Many of the fallen found their final resting place in the field.

Another danger for the assault guns were Russian mine dogs which were trained to run towards tanks. A lever on the animals' backs caused the explosive charges to detonate. The men of the division were forced to kill dogs in general.

The Ausf G was the final version of the assault gun. The initially retained basic armour of 50 mm plus screwed-on 30 mm additional armour was soon to be replaced by a massive 80 mm front plate.

With the beginning of spring, the assault guns, originally delivered in tropical camouflage, were painted darker with camouflage paste. The colour is not known; it could be dark grey (RAL 7021). The vehicle belonged to the 1. Bttr.

In June 1943, the Abteilung was transferred again. This Sturmgeschütz Ausf G could not be repaired in time by the workshop services. The tracks were hastily removed and the vehicle was towed onto an SSys wagon.

JUNE 1943

The months of May and April were characterised by a certain calm. Heeresgruppe Mitte and parts of Heeresgruppe Süd prepared for a large offensive against the Kursk salient. Due to effective intelligence work, the Soviets were fully aware of this danger.

The Soviets reinforced their forces at Kursk thereby weakening the southern part of the Eastern Front. With only occasional artillery strikes and air raids, the German positions from Cherson, Nikopol to Kriwoj Rog (Krywyj Rih) could withstand the reduced enemy pressure.

In this situation StuGAbt 203 was retracted as corps reserve. In a Balka (valley), accommodations were built and the men of the Abteilung could play sports such as handball. Life at the Abteilung became almost idyllic. According to Friedrich Gassauer's memoirs, the men planted vegetable gardens and caught crayfish to supplement their rations.

The new assault guns, which reached the division as replacements, were delivered in dark yellow basic colour (RAL 7028) since April 1943. Camouflage pastes were available to the troops for camouflage. This Ausf G does not yet have Panzerschürzen (side skirts). Smoke candle cups are attached to the front of the superstructure.

In the summer of 1943, Panzerschürzen were introduced on the PzKpfw III and IV as well as on assault guns. These were intended only as protection against fire from anti-tank rifles. On this Ausf G the side skirts were probably retrofitted at the front during the summer. There are 13 kill rings painted on the barrel.

This early Ausf G with bolted additional armour was also retrofitted with armoured skirts. The individual plates were initially suspended from simple brackets. Many were lost in overgrown terrain.

The heavy tractor 18 t (SdKfz 9) was used to tow broken down assault guns. In 1943, the low-bed trailers (SdAnh 116) were no longer in the inventory; they were not up to the poor road conditions on the Eastern Front.

A well-camouflaged assault gun moves slowly through a cornfield. In front of the vehicle an abandoned M3 Stuart can be seen, more enemy tanks are burning on the left.

Soldiers returning from leave in the west of the German Reich brought disturbing news with them. The bombing war against German industry had taken on a terrible form and the population in the cities were suffering greatly.

On 16 June, a handball match took place between two batteries. In the middle of the game, Russian fighter planes attacked. At first the FlaK was able to drive them away but, during further attacks, parts of the shelters were destroyed. The calm was now over. Normal war routine with regular training was resumed.

The officers gave lectures on the combat tactics of assault artillery to other infantry units in order to improve cooperation.

To protect the corps reserve, several artillery positions were set up which regularly opened disruptive fire on the Russian positions.

JULY 1943

From 1 July 1943, Hauptmann Hans Eberhard Handrick took over the command of StuGAbt 203. The officer would also enjoy the short time of peace. However, while carelessly fishing with handgrenades his femoral artery was injured by splinters due to a misfire. The fact that the assistant doctor, Dr Schwarzfischer, was on the spot saved his life.

Operation Zitadelle

The German assault on the Kursk salient by 5 July 1943 marked a further turning point of the war. Four armies (2. and 9 Armee, Armeeabteilung Kempf and 4. Panzerarmee) were fielded. Since the Soviets were well informed it is not surprising that they concentrated large parts of their forces. PzAOK 1, under which Sturmgeschütz-Abteilung 203 fought, was not affected.

On July 7, rumours reached the Abteilung to the effect that the Russians were allegedly preparing a large counterattack, but in the area around Orel. Indeed this large-scale attack was part of the defence battles around Kursk. As a result, the Russian units on the southern front were further thinned out. Here, a deceptive calm spread.

In this situation, the 1. Panzerarmee pointed out that, under the conditions of positional warfare, assault guns must also be used as armoured PaK in prepared firing positions. StuGAbt 203 intervened in sharp form since this deployment was contrary to the operational principles of the assault artillery and would lead to high losses.

However, only short time later the Soviet Southwest Front launched heavy assaults against the German defence lines. From the war diary of 1. Panzerarmee (Pz AOK1):

In the course of the morning it becomes more and more clear that the opponent has now also introduced new mobile forces against the front of the XXIV. PzK. Prisoners' statements confirm that in Northwest Semenivka and at Tscherwonyj Saporoscheza a Russian tank brigade with infantry forces crossed the Donez. Since the early morning hours the enemy has been attacking with strong forces and numerous tanks supported by strong artillery from the forest west of Semenivka. While in the morning all attacks were repulsed, at 15.20 the enemy managed to take Semenivka and to break through to the southwest turning

The Rasputitsa, the mud period, also led to catastrophic conditions in the spring of 1943. This assault gun got stuck in the middle of a village and now has to be recovered at great expense.

to Andreyevka. Here, a battery of StuGAbt 203 and parts of SS-Wiking shot down 28 of 30 tanks. Another attack from the forest west of Semenivka to the south was repelled in the evening. Around 17.00 Saredniy had to be abandoned in view of the superior enemy attack…

This report shows that during a defensive operation a single Sturmgeschütz battery could repel a large Soviet tank assault. In the same file the LVII. PzK reported the destruction of more than 350 tanks in the period from 17 to 22 July 1943, mostly with comparatively few own forces. On the other hand, the overwhelming Soviet materiel superiority is revealed here again. The opponent was apparently always able to make up for his high losses.

For this period the Höheres Artillerie-Kommando (high artillery command) of the 1. Panzerarmee noted in its war diary:

Artillery units destroyed 119 tanks, among them StuGAbt 203 with 10 kills and StuGAbt 232 with 12.

From the summer of 1943, Abteilung 203 introduced specific changes to its assault guns, which make identification easier. This Ausf F/8 was retrofitted in summer 1943 with side skirts whose corners were rounded off with cutting torches. The placement of a spare track roller on the chain cover is also typical. Markings are not visible.

In this context, the war diary of the 1. Panzerarmee (Pz AOK 1) contains an interesting note:

The 46. InfDiv was also constantly knocking down Red attacks against its entire front. However, the loss of strength due to the four days of uninterrupted fighting is considerable, although the division's performance continues to be beyond reproach. The commanding general of the XXXX. Panzerkorps requests the naming of this division in the Wehrmacht report at 18.00 hours. The 46. InfDiv held its main battle line for three days without outside help except for six assault guns of StuGAbt 203 against five enemy rifle divisions, two tank brigades and two independent breakthrough regiments, shooting down over 130 tanks. In the daily report of the Armee, the following sentence shall be included:

The Franconian-Sudeten German 46. InfDiv under its commander GenLt Hauffe had a decisive share in the defensive successes of the last days on the Middle Donez. In the first two days of the battle, the division shot down over 130 enemy combat vehicles with its own weapons, with Uffz Windschütel alone destroying 15 tanks."

By 27 July 1943 the personnel of 2./203 was entirely replaced by a personnel unit from Jüterbog. After some time training, the old soldiers of 2./203, all experienced men, travelled to Altengrabow to form the core of the new Sturmgeschütz unit, StuGAbt 228.

AUGUST 1943

On 3 August, the Soviets launched a further offensive in the Kharkov area, Operation Rumyantsev. Besides the recapture of Belgorod and Kharkov, the aim of the fighting was the annihilation of the 4. German Panzerarmee and Armee-Abteilung Kempf. The attack was made possible by the failure of the German Operation Citadel in the Kursk salient. In the course of 20 days of fighting, the Soviets reconquered Belgorod on 5 August followed by Kharkov on 23 August.

Sturmgeschütz-Abteilung 203 was not directly involved in these decisive battles. Together with the 1. Panzerarmee (Pz AOK 1), the prepared positions south of the city of Voroshilovgrad (Luhansk) were successfully defended. These operations were carried out offensively with the complete Abteilung having its full strength of 31 assault guns.

Subordination Chart
August 1943
HG Süd, Pz AOK 1, XXXX. PzK
StuGAbt 203 attached to 3. PzDiv
3./203 temporarily attached to 15. Inf Div

The 1. Panzerarmee reported the destruction of 133 tanks on 23 August alone. All together the Soviets had lost 501 tanks since 16 August. One day later a further 190 tanks

were destroyed. In the course of the two defensive battles in the Isjum salient, the units attached to the XXXX. Panzerkorps destroyed more than 1000 Russian tanks. These figures again show the great materiel superiority of the Russian armed forces, but they must be viewed with great caution. While the figures themselves are not doubted, any clear allocation of the tank kills to individual German units is impossible.

By 30 August 1943, the enemy launched further assaults at the Stalino (Donezk) front. A breakthrough could only be avoided by mobilization of all the reserves of the XXXX. PzK, including Sturmgeschütz-Abteilung 203.

SEPTEMBER 1943

Subordination Chart
1. September 1943
HG Süd, Pz AOK 1, LVII. PzK
StuGAbt 203 attached to 15. and 328. InfDiv

After the Soviet's successful conclusion of the Fourth Battle of Kharkov, by September 1943, Soviet forces were able to advance westwards on the whole frontline north of Rostov, forcing the German forces to retreat to the west.

By 4 September the 1. Panzerarmee reported 17 Sturmgeschütze to be operational with StuGAbt 203. Other sources note more, possibly by including those in need of repair. The unit lay near Werch Bischkin. In the following battles, the Abteilung was deployed only defensively, but in this role the unit was torn apart more and more often. Battery-wise deployment was the rule but sometimessingle platoons fought. These missions, despite notable occasional successes, were not very effective. The advantage of Sturmgeschütze in combat, especially on the open steppes of southern Russia, could no longer be exploited.

In the southern section of the Eastern Front, an above-average number of English and American tanks sent to Russia under the lend/lease agreement were used by the Red Army. This destroyed M3 A1 was equipped with the 75 mm M3 gun. In the east, the combat value of these tanks was low; for assault guns with a well-rehearsed crew, combat was no problem.

The British Matilda infantry tank was also delivered to the Soviet Union in larger numbers. Although heavily armoured, the armament was below average with the Ordnance 2 Pdr QF (40 mm).

The Matilda was a product of the 1930s. Designed as an infantry tank, it had an armour thickness of up to 80 mm. The rather brittle cast iron armour of the turret and the hull front could however be safely engaged by the PzGr 39 at distances of more than 1000 metres.

As a rule, the fast, offensive and expansive deployment of assault guns in the east was successful. The big obvious disadvantage, the missing rotating turret, could be slightly offset due to the larger battle distances prevailing here where lateral steering movements of the Sturmgeschütze could be reduced to a minimum. Well-trained and well-rehearsed crews (here the cooperation between driver and gunner was decisive) were normally able to cope with the limited lateral traverse of the 7.5 cm Sturmkanone 40.

When used in the defensive role, a skillfully attacking opponent was able to outmanoeuvre the assault guns, especially when these were dug in contrary to the valid German regulations. This applied all the more at low combat strengths and without sufficient flank protection. Every subsequent steering movement cost valuable time. Also, the final drives and brakes, the weak points of the assault guns, were quickly overstressed. Conventional tanks with their rotating turrets were at an advantage here.

Recognizing the retreat operations of the LVII. Panzerkorps, the Soviets launched several attacks against positions near Tschepel by 7 September. Apparently no serious resistance was expected, but the 15. InfDiv, supported by StuGAbt 203, was still in its positions.

Attempts to cross the River Donez here were repulsed.

By 9 September, parts of StuGAbt 203 were deployed near Werch-Bischkin (Verkhny-Bishkin); further forces reached Voroshilovgrad (Luhansk) by 10 to 13 September.

On 15 September, an assault gun slipped sideways while driving over a bridge and crashed into the water. The only crew member, the driver Uffz Müller, survived in an air bubble and was rescued by workshop personnel after four hours. The assault gun could not be recovered and had to be abandoned.

By August the German defenders had received orders to establish a defence line at the River Dnieper, the so-called Ostwall, with the intention to stop the Soviet advance. Due to the little time available it proved impossible to fulfill the high command's wishes, so the defence line remained incomplete.

The Soviets followed the German retreat. The focal points of their effort were Panjutina (Panyutyne) and Lesowaja (Lesowo). The 15. InfDiv annihilated several enemy attacks of regiment strength. Enemy tanks concentrations were recognized at Panjutina.

PzAOK 1's daily strength report dated 16 Sep 1943 shows some inconsistencies. For example, the number of operational assault guns had dropped to eight. No reason for this dramatic development is apparent. Interestingly, according to the report, two of the eight vehicles were assault howitzers. This seems unlikely since the unit was not prepared for this, neither in terms of personnel nor equipment. A conceivable explanation would be a communication error; the "howitzers" could have been 7.5 cm L/24 short barrel guns.

By 21 September the Abteilung reached Dnipropetrovsk (now Dnipro). As important supply facilities were situated in this city, including the K-Werk (a large repair workshop), its loss would be fatal.

On September 24, Russian units of the Southern Front continued to attack towards the Dnieper. From the memories of Friedrich Gassauer:

> We noted an increase in enemy pressure. Apparently reconnaissance missions were ordered by the other side without consideration, it was almost like shooting doves. At 15.00 a Russian fighter plane of the Lag 3 type had to make an emergency landing behind our positions. The plane was seized. The pilot shot himself.

The tank strength of the 1. Panzerarmee was poor. By 22 September, the LVII. Panzerkorps reported that the 23rd PzDiv had eight PzKpfw III (lang), two PzKpfw III (7.5 cm), eight PzKpfw IV (lang) and two PzBefw command tanks. StuGAbt 203 and 232 each had ten Sturmgeschütze, Abteilung 209 seven and 210 eight. For StuGAbt 236 eight Sturmgeschütze und fünf Sturmhaubitzen were reported.

The report proves that other Abteilungen, including "203", were issued at this time only with 7.5 cm Sturmkanone 40 equipped StuGs. The figures quoted above probably only included intact

Parts of StuGAbt 203 on a relocation march. Whenever possible, the tracked vehicles were transported by rail to reduce wear on their vulnerable components. Depending on the traffic, the Panzerschürzen had to be taken down. Here the side skirts remained in place – apparently no oncoming traffic was reported.

On September 15, Heeresgruppe Süd finally began its forced retreat to the western banks of the Dnieper. Within a very short time 63 divisions and all their equipment had to be transferred across only six available bridges spread out on a new front 700 kilometers wide. In addition to about 1 million soldiers, around 200,000 wounded, and just as many civilians plus countless cattle, passed over the crossing points.

and operational vehicles. Abteilungen 209, 210 and 236 were only briefly subordinated to the LVII. tank corps; normally they fought with the XVII. Armeekorps in the 1. Panzerarmee.

During September the Soviets performed various attacks, resulting in their first bridgehead north of the confluence of the Dnieper and Pripyat Rivers by 22 September. Only three days later Dnipropetrovsk was reached. The German units involved here offered heavy resistance.

By 28 September, StuGAbt 203 was transferred to the LII. Armeekorps. This large command level led eight infantry divisions and tank divisions, including the 9. PzDiv and the famous Panzergrenadier-Division "Großdeutschland". By 28 Sep 1943, being attached to the 328. InfDiv, Abteilung 203 had changed its subordination relationship frequently. During its subordination to the LII. AK, StuGAbt 203 is only rarely mentioned in the war diary of the Armeekorps but the reasons for this are unknown. Strength reports were not given.

With combined forces a further counterattack in the bridgehead was launched by 29 September. This attempt was not successful either.

The combat readiness of StuGAbt 203 and all other German units was severely hampered by major supply shortages. On 28 Sep 1943, StuGAbt 232, also assigned to PzAOK 1, reported only three assault guns ready for action. A total of 17 were waiting for replacement engines in the workshop.

Subordination Chart
28. September 1943
HG Süd, Pz AOK 1, LII. PzK
StuGAbt 203 attached to 328. InfDiv

At the end of the month the LII. Armeekorps, and with it StuGAbt 203, had reached the Dnieper. At Nadeshdino a bridgehead was held despite heavy enemy pressure.

OCTOBER 43

Subordination Chart
21. October 1943
HG Süd, Pz AOK 1, LII. PzK
StuGAbt 203 attached to various units

By the beginning of October the unit was again split up. Single batteries with only a few Sturmgeschütze fought under steadily changing subordinations.

Then StuGAbt 203 was deployed around Krivoi Rog. During the heavy fighting, the LVII. PzK reported the attack of Russian forces equipped with captured PzKpfw III tanks mounting 76.2 mm AT guns (SU 76 i). Here the complete unit would be deployed with all remaining operational Sturmgeschütze.

By 11 October, PzAOk 1 sent an alarming message to Heeresgruppe Süd. Due to the "overwhelming" Soviet artillery fire, the personnel losses in the bridgehead at Aporoshje had reached a threatening extent. The general lack of ammunition as well as the lack of replacements of all types of vehicles weighed on the morale of the troops and made the continuation of the fight questionable. The Sturmgeschütz-Abteilungen could only fall back on 13% of the target allocation of ammunition of which only 3% was HE. The decision to abandon the bridgehead had to be made quickly. Moreover, PzAOK 1 doubted that holding the frontline west of the Dnieper was possible with the available forces.

By 11 October, "203" had only three operational Sturmgeschütze. The other, nominally much larger units of the LII. AK did not present a better picture. Thus, the 9. PzDiv only had one PzKpfw IV and the 23. PzDiv had 4 PzKpfw III, 3 PzKpfw IV and one Panther fit for combat.

This unknown lieutenant of StuGAbt 203 shows the silver embroidered epaulettes to the field grey special clothing. The Abteilung´s number (203) was also embroidered; from 1943 this was often missing. As an officer, he wears the typical collar patches with the red piping of the artillery branch.

A non-commissioned officer of the Panzertruppe marvels at the score of this assault gun of StuGAbt 203, more than 15 kill rings are visible on the barrel. The soldier wears the black armour jacket complete with a side cap, plus nondescript camouflage trousers.

Exchanging uniform parts was part of everyday life for soldiers of all nations. This lieutenant has exchanged his headgear for a black side cap of the tank troop.

It is not known whether the exchange of experience between tank troops and assault artillery was welcomed and encouraged. There was certainly no competition. This non-commissioned officer, decorated with the Eisernes Kreuz I. Klasse, inspects an assault gun of the Abteilung with interest. A souvenir photo was important.

In October 1943, the next mud period was approaching. This assault gun was already equipped with V-shaped ice cleats; the camouflage paint is covered by mud, probably the best camouflage. This Ausf G shows a massive 80 mm front armour. The gun mantlet is of the cast-style, sometimes referred to as Saukopf- (pig's head) of Topf- (pot) Blende, so the gun was presumably produced by Alkett. Again spare running wheels have been placed on the track cover.

Despite the presumably low temperatures, the soldiers wear their normal service uniforms; the lieutenant of the assault artillery has additionally procured a fur cap through unofficial channels. The commander's cupola of the Ausf G finally gave the gunner a good all-round view under armour protection.

Close cooperation was essential for the survival of both the assault guns and the infantry. The firepower of the assault guns or Sturmhaubitzen enabled breakthroughs and engaged enemy tanks; the foot soldiers repelled Russian close combatants. Interestingly, Zimmerit was applied to the tank skirts of this assault gun.

By 12 October, the commanding officer of PzAOK 1, GenOb Eberhard von Mackensen, wrote a memo to Heeresgruppe Süd:

As far as I know, the Führer attaches decisive importance to the thorough destruction of the Zaporozhye Dam. The charge will be ready for detonation on 13.10 at 12.00 noon. If I am not given authority to determine the time of ignition, I cannot assume responsibility for the scheduled execution of the destruction. From 1.10 p.m. onwards, the ignition cables may be destroyed or individual parts of the destruction plan may be triggered at any time by enemy fire or air raids. This means that any guarantee is lost that the thoroughly planned destruction will succeed before the enemy reaches the eastern edge of the dam.

signed von Mackensen

This photo proves that low-bed trailers (SdAnh 116) were still available in 1943. They quickly became immobile in the mud. Here, two s ZgKw 18 t (SdKfz 9) were needed to transport a damaged assault gun.

While fierce fighting raged around Dnepropetrovsk, the LII. AK defended a line from Melitpol to Krmentschug on the Dniepr. By 25 October Dnepropetrovsk had to be abandoned. At the end of the month, as the Red Army approached Kiev, von Mackensen was replaced by General der Panzertruppe Hans-Valentin Hube.

Subordination Chart
21. October 1943
HG Süd, Pz AOK 1, LII. PzK
StuGAbt 203 attached to various units

At the beginning of November the Germans reached Alexandrovka and the Dnieper near Augustinovka. Further Soviet attempts to liberate the war-important ore region of Krivoi Rog failed due to the re-establishment German resistance.

By early November 1943, Soviet troops had managed to establish numerous positions 450 kilometers wide and up to about 100 kilometers deep on the western bank of the Dnieper River. The Red Army suffered very high losses in the fighting: more than 1 million soldiers (including 283,000 dead), over 4,000 tanks and 800 airplanes. German losses are not known but they were probably significantly lower.

However, by 7 November 1943 the LVII. PzK (also part of PzAOK 1) sent an alarming notice, making clear the reality of combat in southern Russia:

Losses during the attack of 14. PzDiv

1.) With assault group PzRgt
   Deployed   22 PzKpfw IV lang
   Lost   10, of which 3 were total; 6 in short-term and in 3 long-term repair

2.) With infantry group Bratskij
   Deployed   6 Sturmgeschütze
   Lost   6, 3 of which were total; 2 short-term, 1 long-term repair

3.) With assault group Großdeutschland
   Deployed   6 Sturmgeschütze
   Lost   2, both short-term

Subordination Chart
1 November 1943
HG Süd, Pz AOK 1, LII. AK
StuGAbt 203 attached to various units

The recovery of bogged down assault guns was difficult and time-consuming, but essential in view of the vehicle situation. This work often had to be carried out during the battle under enemy fire. If the recovery failed, the assault guns had to be blown up according to orders.

By 7 November, the LII. Armeekorps had shrunk; only the 3. SS PzDiv "Totenkopf" and the 76. and 384. InfDivs remained subordinated. StuGAbt 203 was the only available assault gun unit.

Since the Dnieper had been crossed by Soviet units at many places, the Abteilung was occasionally deployed to attack these bridgeheads, in most cases with no success. The Soviet pressure was too strong. However, further breakthroughs could be avoided.

From 8 November to 1 December the Abteilung was deployed around Krivoj Rog, 100 km southwest of Dnepropetrovsk. The River Inhulez, a tributary of the Dnieper, served as a further natural obstacle.

Making best use of their weapons, the Abteilung achieved good results.

In November 1943, StuGABt 203 was attached to the 76. InfDiv. During this engagement, Uffz Wilms was to distinguish himself in battle in the area of Konstantinovka north of Stalino (Donetsk). The commander of the 76. InfDiv, General Maximilian de Angelis, reported that:

Unteroffizier (Uffz, sergeant) Wilms, gunner in StuGAbt 203, fought on 14 November 1943 in company with the fusilier regiment 230 and shot down 5 enemy tanks of the type T-34 with his assault gun near Konstantinovka, some of them at the shortest distances. In total he has destroyed 14 tanks lately. I would like to express my appreciation to Uffz Wilms and the men of his gun for this achievement and for their courageous commitment.

Sturmgeschütz-Abteilung 203 would fight until the beginning of December at Krivoi Rog where the Russians had already crossed the Dnieper. In view of the Russian numerical superiority, these fights had only a stalling character and were intended only to delay the Russian advance for as long as possible.

By 14 November the OB (Oberbefehlshaber, commander in chief) of PzAOK 1 submitted a notice to Heeresgruppe Süd explaining the dramatic situation in the following excerpts:

In the heavy defensive battles of the last few weeks, the fighting strength of the army in terms of personnel and materiel has sunk further. Replacement supplies in both areas were only sufficient to fill the very largest gaps in a makeshift manner. The number of well-trained, battle-hardened young officers, subordinate leaders and men has also fallen further...

Due to the total loss of 23,853 men, which was offset by a supply of only 9,410 men, the personnel situation of the army has further deteriorated considerably...

The vehicle situation has also deteriorated dramatically... out of a total of 1321 armoured vehicles, 780 are not operational due to lack of spare parts...

DECEMBER 1943

While StuGAbt 203 remained attached to PzAOK 1, by 10 Dezember a further assault gun unit, StuGAbt 249, was assigned.

Subordination Chart
6 December 1943
HG Süd, Pz AOK 1, LII. PzK
StuGAbt 203 attached to various units

In the course of assault gun production, many technical improvements were made. From March 1943 Alkett, and from July MIAG, introduced massive 80 mm armour on the hull front. This Abt 203 vehicle again shows spare running wheels on the track cover, a modification quite typical for the battalion. A short name is indistinctly visible on the gun mantlet, which has been cleared of snow. A deflector is screwed in front of the first side skirt plate.

By 6 December "203" supported the 384. InfDiv against heavy Soviet attacks. According to Gassauer's recollection, numerous T-34 tanks were destroyed. Two days later, 3. Batterie led a reconnaissance mission against the rail station in Tshabanovka where it was involved in a firefight with twenty Soviet tanks. Four days later, by 10 December, "203" led a counterattack towards Batisman to relieve the divisional command post of the 384. InfDiv, which was attacked by tanks. These battles were successful; furthermore a freight train was recaptured. When the Russians increased their pressure on 13 December, they were repulsed by the 3. Batterie, supported by ME 110 battle planes.

By 17 December parts of StuGAbt 203 formed adhoc Kampfgruppe (battle group) Angelmaier which attacked the train station at Dolinskaia, destroying 13 T-34s and an assault gun without loss.

On 22 December1943, PzAOK 1 reported a great defensive success by StuGAbt 203. By then, 61 tanks, four assault guns, 51 AT guns, four AA guns, one armoured car, eight infantry guns and eight trucks had been destroyed. It remains a mystery how these successes were possible with only three operational Sturmgeschütze.

By 24 December the Soviets launched a further large-scale offensive against the poistions of Heeresgruppe Süd.

The men of StuGAbt 203 celebrated Christmas in Vasilievka. Until the end of the year no more fighting was recorded.

Throughout 1943 StuGAbt 203 had been assigned to PzAOK 1. The fighting in the southern section of the Eastern Front was characterized by continuous retreats. These were mostly planned and could be carried out without heavy personnel losses.

The figures from the daily reports of PzAOK 1 show only the operational assault guns; the number of vehicles in need of repair (but still available) is unknown for the whole of 1943, apart from a few exceptions. By the end of the year, the number of serviceable assault guns had fallen to six.

This photo also reveals the unsatisfactory supply situation in the winter of 1943/44. Despite the cold, these soldiers of StuGAbt 203 are wearing only the normal special clothing. The front armour of the assault gun was apparently "improved" by applying concrete.

These soldiers from StuGAbt 203 are wearing an interesting mix of uniform items. Two reversible winter anoraks are recognisable, one showing the white winter side, the other presumably a splinter camouflage pattern side. The assault gun (Ausf G, Alkett) has been camouflaged in exemplary white.

Fallen comrades were usually buried in larger military cemeteries. Often enough, this was not possible due to the situation at the front.

Losses in combat were negligible; the inability of German industry to supply replacements had a far more dramatic effect. Not even the most important spare parts - engines, side gears and steering brakes - were available in sufficient numbers.

Under these circumstances, the extraordinarily high rate of success of the Sturmgeschütze seems hardly comprehensible. Apart from the daily reports of PzAOK 1, however, no reliable figures are available for the Elefanten-Abteilung.

Because the number of operational assault guns dropped below 10, the division was presumably only suitable for security tasks or attacks with narrowly defined targets.

The situation was similar for the other assault gun divisions of PzAOK 1.

This unknown Oberwachtmeister (sergeant major) of the Abteilung wears only his special clothing despite the spring cold. He was awarded the EK I. (ribbon in buttonhole) and II. Class (pinned cross). He also wears the general assault badge.

STRATEGIC SITUATION IN 1944 THE END OF THE WAR CHAPTER 6

This assault gun Ausf G produced by MIAG shows many interesting details. The return rollers were made entirely from metal to save rubber. Note too that the cover for the sprocket's mounting screws is missing. The large longitudinal rail of the side skirt's mount has been removed; perhaps a rail transport is imminent. Although the photo comes from the estate of a former member of Abt 203, the soldiers are wearing the black uniform jacket of the Panzertruppe.

The Stabsbatterie/StuG Brig 203, led by Lieutenant Wernz, marches to the roll call by the commander of the Sturmgeschütz-Schule Burg, Oberst (Col) Günther Hoffmann-Schönborn. At least one third of the battery wears black uniforms, an indication of supply shortages?

After the Soviet liberation of Kiev, the breakthrough to Zhitomir aiming west could only be stopped by the mobilization of all forces. After Cherkassy was recaptured by 14 December 1943, Soviet forces tried to bypass the positions of the German 8. Armee. By 24 December a major offensive was launched heading northwest and south. This successful advance menaced the left flank of Heeresgruppe Süd. If the Soviet plan of attack was successful, all German troops between the Dnieper and Dniester were threatened with being cut off. The crisis of Heeresgruppe Süd became even more problematic when the Soviets started to attack the lower Dnieper arc at Nikopol and Krivoi Rog.

By 7 January the Soviets began building up a pocket around Cherkassy. Here six German divisions were encircled in the area of Korsun and Boguslav. A relief attack was launched by 11 February. Ignoring Hitler's strict orders, von Manstein instructed German units to evacuate the pocket. Leaving all materiel behind, some 40,000 men managed to escape.

In the southern sector the Soviet forces launched an offensive on 30 January in the direction of Nikopol. In the course of the Russian Kirovograd operation in mid-January, the 8. Armee was forced to withdraw from the Kirovograd area. Now that the flank of the 6. Armee (Army Group A, v. Kleist) was threatened, which on Hitler's order was still defending the industrial area of Nikopol - Krivoy Rog - Kherson, the German

In May 1944, the Abteilung, now called Sturmgeschütz-Brigade 203, was transferred to Burg near Magdeburg for refreshment. Here the unit was equipped according to the new KStN 446 with ten assault guns per battery. For the first time, 10.5cm assault howitzers were also assigned.

units had to give up city by city. Hitler could not accept this defensive approach so he dropped von Manstein and von Kleist at the end of March and transferred them to the Führer reserve. In their place, Walter Model and Ferdinand Schörner took command of the newly formed army groups Nordukraine and Südukraine. By 22 February Krivoi Rog was taken. At this time, the pressure on the south of the Eastern Front decreased as the Soviets were now pulling together all available forces to carry out Operation Bagration, which would annihilate Heeresgruppe Mitte, which at this point in time was still deep inside Soviet territory.

Twelve German divisions, among them three Panzer-Divisions, were shattered leaving only a few remnants.

These new assault guns are of Alkett manufacture, as evidenced by the typical Zimmerit covering and the cast gun mantlet. The side skirt plates are attached to an improved suspension with triangular plates.

Sergeants Mößinger, Gemecker and Hump in July 1944, shortly before transfer to the Eastern Front. The men of the brigade were accommodated privately. This photo was taken in Theesen near Burg.

Lieutenant Wernz in May 1944. The officer is wearing the normal service dress.

On 27 July 1944, the brigade was loaded near the Altengrabow military training area. Here you can see parts of the supply train, modern all-terrain trucks of the type Büssing-NAG 4500 A.

On 31 July 1944, Tauroggen was reached and the brigade was unloaded here. The new assault guns already showed the first typical conversions, for example replacement running wheels were mounted on the front of the chain cover.

After production at Alkett in Berlin-Borsigwalde, the new assault guns were transferred to the Magdeburg Heereszeugamt (army depot) where they were equipped with radios. After completion, Brigade 203 took over the vehicles.

JANUARY 1944

For StuGAbt 203 the short rest period was to last until January 1944. On 1 January, a tragic event shook the 1. Bttr. A soldier suffered a nervous breakdown and killed three of his comrades with a pistol, whereupon he was also shot.

At the beginning of 1944, Sturmgeschütz-Abteilung 203 left its assignment under PzAOK 1 and was transferred to AOK 8. During this time, parts of the Abteilung were temporarily subordinated to the 76. InfDiv.

According to a note attributable to Heeresgruppe Süd, "203" had the following strengths on the dates shown. This note shows the discrepancy between operational assault guns and those in need of repair:

Operational state of StuGAbt 203

	operational	short term repair	long term repair
3 January 1944	5	18	1
11 January 1944	2	12	1

On 5 January 1944, the LII. Armee-Korps reported eight operational assault guns each for StuGAbt 203 and 286. For an unspecified period of time, the destruction of 93 Russian tanks was noted.

Subordination Chart
5 January 1944
HG Süd, AOK 8, LII. AK
StuGAbt 203 attached to 76. InfDiv

On 11 January at about 4 am, 3./203 was ordered to Narovka. At 6 am the attack on the village began in cooperation with elements of the 355. InfDiv. After taking the

New armoured skirts were made using the original parts. The former rigid brackets were removed. Steel plates were fixed to the superstructure, in the area of the undercarriage they were suspended oscillating from the track covers.

village the Russians made a counterattack and Narovka fell into Russian hands again. One assault gun was lost and burnt out.

When a further platoon of assault guns under OLt Stollmann intervened in the fighting, the Russians were thrown back once more – the usual folly of war.

Until 17 January the 3. Bttr remained in Narovka for security purposes. In the evening hours the entire Abteilung transferred to the 320. InfDiv.

On 18 January, the number of operational Sturmgeschütze had dropped to seven; StuGAbt 203 was now attached to the 11. PzDiv.

Subordination Chart
13 January 1944
HG Süd, AOK 8, Armeegruppe Wöhler
StuGAbt 203 attached to various InfDiv

Shortly after arriving in Tauroggen (East Prussia), the brigade went into battle. The brackets of the tank skirts had proved insufficient in earlier missions, a commonly known problem. This vehicle already shows traces of shelling on the skirts – the supports are bent. The front of the superstructure was covered with a thick layer of concrete. Further conversions will follow.

FEBRUARY 1944

This Opel Blitz 3.6-36 S carried the brigade's field kitchen. For this purpose, a wooden superstructure was mounted on the platform according to a proven pattern and an effective, three-colour, camouflage paint applied. Again, the diversity of the uniforms is striking.

At the beginning of February the weather changed again with the thaw making all roads impassable. By 13 February the Generalkommando of the XXXXVII. Panzerkorps sent a call for help to the high command of the 8. Army (AOK 8):

To AOK 8

During the heavy hard fighting the combat readiness of 3., 11., 13. and 14. Panzerdivisions was severely reduced by the steady operation and attacks in the mud. Men and materiel have been consumed to a degree hitherto unknown to me.

1.

The regiments, whose combat strength have sunk to a level of around 200 men, are beginning to become completely apathetic due to overexertion. Since the roads can no longer be used for tracked vehicles, their supply is still encountering difficulties. The Panzergrenadiers are forced to fight almost without heavy weapons.

2.

Panzer and SPW move in the muddy terrain with a speed of 2 to 3 km/h. The running wheels jam, tracks and engines suffer greatly. Consequently most of our Panzer, SPW and Sturmgeschütze lie immobilized by deep mud on the access routes. Their recovery is impossible due to the lack of tractors, as is the towing of the stuck wheeled vehicles. The dramatic losses of tractors make any change of position of the artillery impossible at present.

3.

The number of broken-down motor vehicles is already so great that the above-mentioned divisions will only be ready for use again as fast units after a longer break and after an abundant supply of equipment and spare parts, even if the road conditions improve.

4.

Despite all attempts to sharply concentrate all available forces, the units available at the Hauptkampflinie (HKL, main line of resistance), especially west of Lipyanka, are in no way adequate. If the Russians let our men and materiel continue to detoriate in the mud, and if he attacks himself when the weather improves, we will not be able to resist these attacks with the available forces.

5.

The ordered attack will continue on 14 February, with all forces being combined.

The pendulum skirts had the advantage that they did not snag and tear off when hitting obstacles. These conversions were carried out in a similar way by many other StuG brigades, a sign that suggestions for improvement were passed on.

This was the brigade commander's assault gun. The four-digit tactical number cannot be explained. Possibly this served to confuse the enemy. The advantages of the new skirt suspension are obvious.

It is not surprising that the commander of the XXXXVII. Armeekorps names only its nominally most powerful units, that is to say the Panzer divisions. Sturmgeschütz-Abteilungen as support units at an army level were possibly too small to mention as they were subordinated at battalion level. It is, however, obvious that StuGAbt 203 was also affected by these problems.

Under these circumstances the German forces in southern Russia were hardly capable of operational-tactical operations.

By 1 February, StuGAbt 203 retreated further to the west, towards the River Bug. The unit moved into new accommodation at the Bratske collective farm. Friedrich Wernz notes in his memories:

The road conditions were indescribable. All attempts to send our Sturmgeschütze into action ended up with vehicles getting stuck in the tough mud and breaking down… By 18 February the winter broke in once again with full force. Extremely violent snowstorms raged on the steppe. The drifts are so strong that the roads are still unusable. Today a sergeant had to fetch fuel from our immobilized supply train, he organized ten panje horse teams with sledges and covered a distance of over 50 km. … By 22 February the Stabs-Batterie (staff battery) left Bratske. The new destination, Novo Ukrainka, was reached by 25 February. During the transfer the Stabs-Batterie left nearly all wheeled vehicles behind because of fuel shortage or technical damage. All lost vehicles were blown up."

The crews used their discretionary powers and very different solutions emerged. This Ausf G from the Alkett production line was equipped with a remote-controlled machine gun. The machine gun is vaguely visible, but the armoured shield is missing

Organizational changes - StuG units with 45 Sturmgeschütze

By October 1943, the Organisationsabteilung reported its plans to increase the number of Sturmgeschütze per unit. These plans envisaged bringing all 42 Sturmgeschütz divisions to a strength of 45 Sturmgeschütze until end of 1944.

As a command assault gun, Nr "2001" was equipped with a powerful radio system. Besides the normal Fu 16 radio set (range approx. 4-6 km), an Fu 8 set with a range of up to 40 km was available. This was operated with a star antenna which is visible at the rear of the superstructure.

However, due to the tense production situation, the Sturmartillerie received at that time only 52% of the Sturmgeschütz output. All remaining vehicles were issued to Panzer and PzGren units, and in increasing numbers to Panzerjäger units of army units (Inf Div, JgDiv, GebDiv) and Luftwaffe field divisions. Thus by end of 1943 it was decided to raise the number of Sturmgeschütze from 31 to 45 only for selected units, and only in the case of new establishments or refurbishments.

First Lieutenant Wernz on a test drive with a VW Type 166 Schwimmwagen. Also called VW-Schwimmer, this versatile vehicle was not much more expensive to produce than a sidecar bike. The rifle mount holds an MP 44, probably the best infantry weapon of the 2. World War.

These organizational changes did not concern Sturmgeschütz-Abteilung 203. The authorized strength was still 31 StuG (at that time still without Sturmhaubitzen). However, the stock of operational vehicles during combat at the Dnieper front decreased continuously.

By February/March 1944 it was decided to rename all formations being provided with Sturmgeschütze. This was possibly done to ease differentiation between Sturmartillerie units (Heerestruppe) and other branches. The Organisations-Abteilung (organizational department) decreed in a document dated 29 February 1944:

To be renamed while maintaining their current KStN organization and subordinations:

a) *Sturmgeschütz-Abteilungen (Heerestruppe) to Sturmgeschütz-Brigade*
b) *Panzerjäger-Kompanien (Sturmgeschütz) within PzJgAbt of Infanterie, Jäger- and Gebirgs-Divisionen to Sturmgeschütz-Abteilung*
c) *independent Sturmgeschütz-Batterien within divisions to Sturmgeschütz-Abteilung*

The following units will not be renamed:

d) *Sturmgeschütz-Abteilungen which are permantly attached to divisions.*
e) *Panzer-Abteilungen (Sturmgeschütz), which are permanently attached to divisions*

The crew of an assault gun, late in the year 1944. The comrade on the left seems a little too tall for the small Sturmgeschütz. The top hat and bowler hat were certainly not covered by any regulation. In the background is a damaged vehicle without a track.

As a former Heerestruppe unit, StuGAbt 203 now received the new name Sturmgeschütz-Brigade (StuGBrig 203). The formerly authorized strength remained untouched.

MARCH 1944

By March 1944, StuGAbt 203 changed its designation to Sturmgeschütz-Brigade (StuGBrig) 203. However, for the "Elephants" nothing changed. Apart from the occasional delivery of replacements, the unit did not receive any further reinforcements.

Again from the memories of Friedrich Wernz:

> By 2 March we again retreated to the west. The thaw made all movements almost impossible. On the unmetalled roads our vehicles sank in the mud up to their axles. After a day and a half we reached our new destination, a village 15 km west from Novo Arkhangelsk. Our brigade was in a very bad condition, we were barely able to keep our assault guns operational. To make matters worse, Russian low-flying planes shot one of our trucks on fire…

> Retreating further in southwest direction: by 14 March the brigade ran short of fuel. The Stabsbatterie reached the village of Sumilovka with the last drop. Luckily we found a deserted truck with 400 l of petrol. This was enough to reach the bridge crossing the River Bug.

Subordination Chart
14 March 1944
HG Süd, AOK 8, Armeegruppe Wöhler
StuGBrig 203 attached to 13. PzDiv

During the whole of March, the entire army group was on the retreat, with the remains of StuGAbt 203 in the middle. One of the few surviving Sturmgeschütze was in constant use pulling stuck vehicles through the sludge.

Finally, on 29 March 1944 at 11.00 in the morning, the Dniester was reached and crossed. All roads and villages to the west were full of vehicles and soldiers. StuGAbt 203 had reached Bessarabia.

Friedrich Wernz noted this in his memoirs that, although being well received and cared for, the customs and behaviour of the local population needed getting used to.

Not all assault guns of the brigade could be equipped with the improved side skirt mountings. This Sturmhaubitze carried the 10.5 cm StuH 42, an effective gun for engaging soft and hard targets.

APRIL 1944

By 17 April the remains of StuGBrig 203 gathered in a wine village. The unit's replenishment at home in the Reich was already decided. In this situation the brigade's commander, General Schörner, issued orders to the XXXXVII. Panzerkorps:

StuGBrig 203 will be released from the front. The remaining assault guns, all equipment including motor vehicles will be handed over to StuGBrig 905. The personnel of the unit are to be deployed to Braila for refreshment. The brigade will be placed under the command of the Army Group South Ukraine.

Army Group Wöhler High Command

By 20 May the unit was ordered to Braila, a small city on the River Danube.

MAY 1944

Now promoted to first lieutenant, Friedrich Wernz is sitting here in the battery officer's Kfz 70. In the spacious rear of the heavy off-road Steyr 1500 car, the empty frames of the radio equipment are visible, so the car has been converted into a radio vehicle (Kfz 15).

Men of the brigade in a VW Schwimmwagen. Well camouflaged in the forest stands a Sturmgeschütz. The highly manoeuvrable amphibious vehicle was fully equal to the difficult terrain in the east. Hptm Lembke is visible sitting in the vehicle. OLt Angelmaier holds his service cap in his hand. The capable officer was to take over command of StuG Brig 279 in October 1944.

On 4 May 1944 the personnel of StuGBrig 203 were ordered to Braila train station. The following day, the journey home began via Buzan, Ploieşti, Kronstadt, Budapest, Vienna, Brünn, Breslau, Dresden, Berlin and finally Burg near Magdeburg.

The personnel were given home leave while the new establishment was being prepared. From mid-June, first the officers and then the enlisted men returned.

Re-establishment

The re-establishment took place at the Altengrabow military training area. The crews were accommodated in Krüssau near Burg.

StuGBrig 203 was established according the current organizational structures. Since in the meantime it had become clear that the planned increase from 31 StuG per brigade to 45 for all units was out of reach so the respective KStN 446a (31 StuG) and 446b (45 StuG) were combined. The new KStN 446 dated 1 June 1944 was relevant for batteries authorized to have 10 or 14 Sturmgeschütze. Compared to the older structure, the number of soft-skinned vehicles was substantially reduced – a hint of the further worsening supply situation.

- KStN 446 StuGBttr with 10 or 14 Geschütze dated 1 June 1944 (for "203" 10 StuG were authorized).
- KStN 416 Stab and Stabsbatterie dated 1 June 1944.

For the first time Sturmhaubitzen, assault howitzers mounting the 10.5 cm StuH 42, were issued besides the 7.5 cm StuK 40 armed Sturmgeschütz. Thus the unit received 22 Sturmgeschütz Ausf G and nine Sturmhaubitze Ausf G.

The three formerly independent trains were combined in one Abteilungs-Tross. Since motorcycles proved to be unsuited for use on the Eastern Front, their number was significantly reduced. These were partly substituted by half-tracked Kettenkrads (SdKfz 2) and light Kübelwagen cross-country cars. The staff battery received two VW Schwimmwagen, vehicles most welcomed because of their usefulness for reconnaissance duties. On the whole the number of soft-skinned vehicles remained similar. To meet the terrain problems, two le ZgKw 1 t (SdKfz 10) halftracks were issued.

The ammo trucks of the Gefechtsbatterie were deleted and combined into a smaller ammo section, all in all seven trucks could be saved. A Kettenkrad and a VW Schwimmwagen were also stricken off the roll. The reduction to three combat platoons was insignificant, since it was always within the brigade commander's competence to restructure his unit.

On 30 August 1944, a delegation of the brigade visited the Wolfsschanze, the Führer's headquarters near Rastenburg. The reason is not known, possibly OLt Angelmaier (3rd from left) was decorated by the Führer Adolf Hitler.

September 1944. First Lieutenant Wernz (left) in front of his Chef-Geschütz, a StuG Ausf G of Alkett manufacture. This assault gun was also still equipped with the regular side skirts. The remote control MG usually provided for the loading gunner is missing, presumably due to the usual lack of parts.

As for the StuG units issued at Heerestruppen level, the situation would become even more complicated by June 1944, after Begleit-Batterien (escort batteries) were issued to selected StuG units. The units were again re-named:

- Sturmgeschütz-Brigaden without Begleit-Batterien received the designation: Heeres-Sturmgeschütz-Brigade

- Sturmgeschütz-Brigaden with Begleit-Batterien received the designation: Heeres-Sturmartillerie-Brigade

These were Heeres-StuArtBrig 236, 239 and 667.

The new designations did not necessarily give hints to the actual authorized strength. In principle a Sturmgeschütz unit could have 22, 31 or 45 Sturmgeschütze because the older KStN 446 and 446a were still valid.

The 'Elephant Brigade' now had the official designation Heeres-Sturmgeschütz-Brigade 203 (HStuGBrig).

Change of vehicle markings

With the re-establishment, the brigades' numbering system was changed. Until the end of 1943, the four batteries were distinguished by a clear colour marking of the heraldic animal, the elephant. The vehicles themselves were clearly distinguished within the batteries by a two-digit number, usually stencilled in white. Since the brigade was often subordinated to different divisions in batteries, there were presumably no problems.

The staff and staff battery of a Sturmgeschütz-Brigade was also changed to fit the size of the unit (KStN 416 dated 1 June 1944). If the combat batteries were authorized with 14 Sturmgeschütze, the brigade staff received two additional StuGs and the supply echelon one further fuel truck.

By 1 July 1944 only five units - StuGBrig 191, StuGBrig 279, StuGBrig 259, StuGBrig 341 and StuGBrig 303 - were authorized to have 45 StuGs per Abteilung. Accordingly all remaining Sturmgeschütz units including StugBrig 203 were authorized to have 31 StuGs per Abteilung.

Unfortunately, there are only very few significant photos of the brigade from the time 1944/45. Therefore, it is not possible to definitively answer the question of the new marking system.

In fact, the author is only aware of one photo of an assault gun that can be clearly assigned to the brigade and was also marked with a number. This vehicle, a Sturmhaubitze, bears the number "2001", curiously a four-digit number. Since this vehicle is a command assault gun, it could be the assault gun of the brigade commander Hptm Jandrik. Why a four-digit number was used, and why it begins with a "2" cannot be explained.

All other known photos of assault guns of Sturmgeschütz-Brigade 203 show no markings except for the nationality mark, the Balkenkreuz. Often enough this is also missing. The typical elephant symbol is also missing.

These open questions still need to be answered.

Modification of the vehicles
Assault gun units often modified their assault guns to suit their specific needs. It is interesting to note that this was done on a much larger scale than, for example, with units of the Panzertruppe. One possible explanation would be the relatively small size of the assault gun brigades.

These modifications and improvements included, for example, equipping the vehicles with large wooden boxes to give the crew the opportunity to stow their personal belongings.

A well-known weak point of the assault guns was the delicate suspension of the side Panzerschürzen (side skirts). When driving in rough terrain, tree stumps could be touched. Individual plates could be lifted off and were then often permanently lost.

Resourceful assault gun soldiers devised a remedy. Smaller segments were cut from the existing plates, which were then suspended pendulously from the track cover plates. The remains of the plates were mounted on the superstructure at an angle. These solutions could be realized by the workshop platoons themselves. The pendulum skirts were to prove themselves well; on contact with solid obstacles, they swerved backwards and then swung back to their original position.

Via the assault artillery school in Burg, these suggestions for improvement were collected and forwarded to other units.

During August, fighting blazed around the East Prussian village of Wilkowischken. Parts of Brigade 203 supported the defensive fight of the PzGrenDiv "Großdeutschland".

In early summer, the Elephant Brigade converted a number of its assault guns accordingly, resulting in different solutions.

In July 1944, the Panzerregiment "Großdeutschland" had 77 modern tanks of the type "Panther" at its disposal, about half of which were ready for action. StuG Brig 203 took over the important flank protection during the defensive battles around Wilkowischken. The battery officer's car is visible on the left.

JULY 1944

In the second half of July 1944, it was decided to send HStuGBrig 203 to the area of Army Group North.

In the early morning hours of 27 July, the brigade received orders to load for transport to the next deployment. Due to many problems, the loading of all parts lasted until 22.00 in the evening. On 28 July, the brigade left Altengrabow.

The march led via Küstrin an der Oder, Landsberg an der Warthe (Gorzów Wielkopolski) firstly to Schneidemühl (Piła). On 29 July the journey continued via intermediate stations in Elbing (Elbląg), Braunsberg (Braniewo) and Königsberg (Kaliningrad) and Tilsit. Here the 3. Bttr with its new chief Hptm Lembke was stopped. Initially, the brigade was to continue to Tauroggen (Tauragé). Due to the situation, however, the brigade was transported again southwest to Insterburg (Wolodino), where it was finally unloaded on 31 July.

The assault howitzers were equipped with hollow charge projectiles, which also made it possible to fight against enemy tanks. With overall poor accuracy, its use was possible up to 1,500m; up to 100 mm steel could be penetrated.

This Sturmhaubitze also still shows the regular side skirts. The armoured vehicle was very well camouflaged in a forest.

Despite its cramped interior, the VW Schwimmwagen was a very popular vehicle. The commander of the brigade preferred it to the heavier vehicles. Hptm Handrick is visible on the left; the brigade's Spieß is on the right.

AUGUST 1944

Combat in Wilkowischken

Subordination Chart
2 August 1944
HG Mitte, PzAOK 3, XXXX. PzK
StuGBrig 203 attached to 561. VGrenDiv

The brigade commander, Hans Eberhard Handrick, was promoted to major in autumn 1944. To his left is First Lieutenant Wernz, by now head of the 1. Bttr.

Army Group North, which had reached Leningrad in 1941, had been involved in heavy infighting ever since. Significant gains in terrain could not be achieved; the enemy defended its homeland tenaciously.

In the shadow of a small church near Wilkowischken are several assault guns of the brigade. The Sturmhaubitze shows no side skirts and no mountings on the superstructure.

When Heeresgruppe Mitte (Army Group Centre) collapsed at the end of June 1944, the situation in the former Baltic states would be affected. Now the southern wing of Army Group North was unprotected in the Polozk area and the 16. Armee (General der Infantry Paul Laux) had to retreat along the Düna River towards Riga.

The western part of the still-occupied Baltic states now came under the purview of the newly reformed Heeresgruppe Mitte. At the end of July and beginning of August 1944, fierce battles raged in the immediate vicinity of the town of Wilkowischken (Vilkaviškis). The Red Army approached the German pre-war border directly here for the first time. In the first days of August, the Germans once again managed to recapture the town.

By 2 August Heeres-Sturmgeschütz-Brigade 203 actively intervened in the fighting. Already on 1 August, the third battery recorded eight kills, including the heaviest tank types (JS II). In the following days, another 26 tanks were shot down.

This assault howitzer serves as transport for a group of grenadiers in autumn 1944. Interestingly, an MG 42 was mounted behind the protective shield instead of the standard MG 34. No side plates were attached to the superstructure. The 10.5cm StuH 42 seems to have been replaced; the barrel and muzzle brake show a different paint job.

On 6 August, a Sturmgeschütz of Brigade 203 mistakenly took a Tiger of PzGrenDiv "GD" under fire and as a result the heavy tank had to be written off as a total loss. The corps headquarters of the XXVI. Armeekorps initiated a court martial investigation.

On 12 August 1944 orders were given to prepare the bridges in Wilkowischken for demolition.

The defence of the village succeeded with great difficulty. PzGrenDiv "Großdeutschland", which also fought here, suffered heavy losses. In total, the unit lost four PzKpfw IV, 14 PzKpfw V and five PzKpfw VI on 9 and 10 August 1944. After combat, these total losses were attributed to:

- The complete domination of the airspace by the enemy.
- Strong superiority, as well as the rapid approach of, the enemy's anti-tank reserves.
- The heavily overgrown terrain unsuitable for Panzer operations.
- The use of a new type of heavy PaK in great numbers, which was able to penetrate Panther and Tiger at the first hit and cause immediate burnouts.

According to the report, these losses were offset by 71 Russian tanks and over 100 guns destroyed by German units. The ominous new PaK could not be identified. In all probability, it was the 100 mm BS 3 which appeared in August 1944.

The StuGbrig 203 was apparently deployed defensively; as late as October, the unit reported 29 operational Sturmgeschütze.

By 13 August HStuGBrig 203 retreated to Wirballen (Virbalis). Two days later PzAOK 3 reported in its daily report:

South of the river Memel, after 45 minutes of heavy artillery preparatory fire, the enemy attacked the East Prussian border at noon with parts of 6 - 7 rifle divisions and two armoured brigades under continuous use of combat aircraft on a broad front. In the north of Wilkowischken, he succeeded in making several breakthroughs on both sides of the railway line...

Since the summer of 1944, the heavy Russian JS-IIs had been in action on the Eastern Front. For the assault guns, the well-armoured tanks were a tough opponent. Combat was practically only possible from the side.

On 17 August 1944, Wilkowischken was finally taken by the Red Army and PzAOK reported succinctly:

... The enemy continued his attacks on the Reichsgrenze (German border) on both sides of Wilkowischken. The town itself was lost during the night...

During the following months, the front line moved back and forth in the immediate vicinity of the town. While the Russian attackers had apparently sufficient reserves, the German units became weaker and weaker, but continued fighting with the greatest determination. The Sowjets were at the gates of Ostpreußen!

The different Heeres-Sturmgeschütz units involved in the sector of PzAOK 3 (brigades 203, 232, 276 and 277) were in comparably good condition in the last quarter of 1944. The materiel state of HStuGBrig 203 is evident by its strength table.

Subordination Chart

23 August 1944

HG Mitte, PzAOK 3, XXVI. AK

StuGBrig 203 attached to 561. VGrenDiv

3./StugBrig 203 attached to 6. PzDiv

Subordination Chart

28 August 1944

HG Mitte, PzAOK 3, XXVI. AK

StuGBrig 203 army troop

3./StugBrig 203 attached to 549. VGrenDiv

SEPTEMBER 1944

Along the entire frontline from Riga via Schaulen, Kaunas and Suwalki to Bialystok, the Soviets attacked incessantly with strong forces. In order to fight the numerous breakthroughs, the remnants of all units had to be thrown from combat to combat. At first, the Soviets established points of main effort to overcome the River Memel (Njemen). As strong as the Russian attacks were, Heeresgruppe Mitte was able to hold this line for a long time.

In late autumn 1944, the brigade was able to report the confirmed shooting down of the 1,000th enemy tank since the beginning of the Russian campaign. The Sturmhaubitze is equipped with conventional side skirts; the superstructure front was apparently reinforced with concrete.

Men of StuG Brig 203 proudly present themselves in front of their prey, a JS-II M. The track seems to be shot into pieces, possibly the immobilized heavy tank could be fought from the side and destroyed. Again, the mix of uniforms is striking.

Subordination Chart

2 September 1944

HG Mitte, PzAOK 3, XXVI. AK

StuGBrig 203 attached to 561 GrenDiv

3./StugBrig 203 to 549. VGrenDiv

The VW Schwimmwagen was rarely used to cross water obstacles. Unlike the Kübelwagen, the vehicle had all-wheel drive. In combination with its low weight it had an exceptional off-road capability. The car is marked with the new tactical sign for assault guns.

Throughout the winter, the German units doggedly defended east of Königsberg – the Soveit troops had to pay dearly for every meter. In the meantime Heeresgruppe Nord was trapped in Kurland (Courland).

HStuGBrigade 203 also suffered losses in these battles. On 7 September, Captain Lembke, commander of 3./203, fell. His post was taken over by Lt Wörner.

The heavy Russian JSU-152s were relatively immobile and had only insufficient means of observation. The much more manoeuvrable assault guns mostly tried to catch them sideways. This vehicle, once bogged down, became easy prey.

OKTOBER 1944

By 11 October, the 549. VGrenDiv was transferred from the XXVI. Armeekorps to the XXVII. Armeekorps, together with 3./H StuGBrig 203.

Subordination Chart
21 Oct – 2 Nov 1944
HG Mitte, AOK 4, XXVI. AK
StuGBrig 203 attached 561. VGrenDiv
HG Mitte, AOK 4, XXVII. AK
3./StugBrig 203 attached to 549. VGrenDiv

On 15 October 1944, the OK PzAOK 3 reported the situation:

After the failure of the attempted breakthrough on Tilsit and the lower reaches of the Memel, the enemy has temporarily switched to defence. In front of the positions of our 3. Panzerarmee, the Soviets have deployed the 2. Guards Army and the I. Panzer Corps. The enemy is expecting further fresh forces.

After the arrival of Fallschirm-Panzerkorps "HG" the 3. Panzer-Armee is able to resist further Russian attacks. However, when the Russians receive the expected reserves, the situation changes.

On 23 October, the 549. VGrenDiv led a counterattack on Ebenrode (Nesterov) with the attached 3. Batterie of HStuGBrig 203. Again, the front could be stabilized for a short time and the remnants of GrenRgt 912 entrenched themselves with some assault guns in Tiefenfeld. Enemy assembly areas could be smashed by the German artillery. In the evening the division reported two tank kills, bringing the number of tanks destroyed since 16 October 1944 to 74.

In the following days the enemy increased their pressure and the 549. VGrenDiv, supported by 3./H StuGBrig 203, had to fight enemy tanks that had broken through in close combat.

portion of tanks in need of repair is incomparably higher than that of the assault guns. This discrepancy cannot be explained. Possibly this was due to the different operational doctrine.

The available strength reports show that of all the Sturmgeschütz-Brigaden deployed in the area of PzAOK 3, StuG-Brig 203 was still the best positioned. While "203" still had 18 operational StuG on 25 October, brigades 232, 277 and 276 had 16, 15 and 6 combat vehicles respectively.

In view of the situation, PzAOK 3 was sent a list of facilities and objects in East Prussia to be prepared for destruction on 24 October. In addition to bridges, this list included factories, dairies, sawmills, waterworks, mills, publishing houses, slaughterhouses, gas and electricity plants and even a knacker's yard.

This scorched earth policy was the admission of the lost war.

On 25 October, PzAOK 3 complained of a decline in its own fighting strength. As a result of the terrain losses, some of them considerable, the morale of the troops sank. It was emphasized that the fight against the Soviets had to be continued with the utmost doggedness.

Part of the brigade was deployed during the battles for Königsberg in the winter of 1944/45. During the hasty retreat across the Frische Haff, the vehicles were left behind, apparently without being blown up.

A strength report dated 23 October shows that 203's operational strength had again dropped significantly, worsening the situation. It is noteworthy that the complete PzAOK 3 reported for the 23 October; 22 operational tanks (and 60 in repair) and 121 operational Sturmgeschütze (103 in repair) (the assault gun numbers included Jagdpanzer IVs and Hetzers).

These figures show that towards the end of the war the production of turretless assault guns clearly exceeded that of conventional tanks. It is interesting to note that the pro-

One day later, the supreme commander of PzAOK 3, Generaloberst Raus, pointed out the general shortage of fuel.

However, the general retreat was a reality. Towards the end of October, the front had to be taken back further to the west where a defensive position between Memel (Klaipeda) and Insterburg (Chernyakhovsk) was prepared.

The German Propaganda was in full swing, as a contemporary press report attests:

In nine days of bloody fighting, the Soviets, attacking from the Wilkowischken area, were only able to reach a depth of 12 or 15 km in the East Prussian area. Hundreds of tanks, thousands of dead lie on the battlefield. Prisoner testimonies confirm Stalin's plan to tear open East Prussia up to the Vistula in a rapid breakthrough in order to collapse the German front in the east... The German countermeasures in the area of Gumbinnen and Goldap, but at the same time also the sustained resistance of the Grenadier and Volksgrenadier divisions in the area of Wilkowischken and Ebenrode, have frustrated the Soviet plan... More than 800 tank wrecks.... show that Stalin's plan has failed.

There is nothing to add to this report.

On 29 October 1944, PzAOK 3 ordered the formation of grenadier escort trains for assault gun and fighter tank units following instructions of the OB of Heeresgruppe Mitte:

Experience has shown time and again that wherever assault guns have been used in close cooperation with infantry, decisive successes in attack and defence could be achieved even with small forces... Assault guns must not be deployed alone in any phase of a battle.

In order to ensure that this requirement is met uniformly, it is ordered that Begleit-Grenadier-Züge be established...

This directive was based on the generally known sensitivity of assault guns to lateral fire and leaked enemy tank destruction commands. The deployment of Begleit-Grenadier-Züge (escort grenadier platoons), which served only for close protection of the valuable assault guns, was a logical consequence. The above order was directed only at

This late StuG Ausf G (Alkett) already shows no Zimmerit covering. Armour plates were still mounted on the superstructure – these are missing on the hull. A hit can be seen on the 80 mm front plate, which bounced off without causing much damage.

Infanterie, Grenadier and Volksgrenadier-divisions that had organic Sturmgeschütz or Jagdpanzer companies (10 or 14 vehicles). These large units also had the possibility to set up escort grenadier platoons from their own resources.

However, Sturmgeschütz-Brigaden of the artillery were independent units being attached at corps or army level (Heerestruppen). These were temporarily subordinated to the larger units (divisions) of the corps or army, often for only a few days.

The Elephant Brigade, which was re-established in mid 1944 as a Heeres-Sturmgeschütz-Brigade, had no own organic Grenadier-Begleitkompanien. Only three Sturmartillerie units, Heeres-Sturmartillerie-Brigade 236, 239 and 667 (each having 45 StuG) could be issued with organic escort batteries.

A further four Sturmgeschütz-Brigaden (177, 189, 270 and 394) having 31 StuG were steadily attached to larger mother units, i.e. divisions. These units also received escort platoons.

HStuGBrig 203 was never issued with organic Begleit-Grenadiere, and was thus dependent on allocations by the divisions to which they were currently assigned. This cooperation was not always successful because the individual subunits were not attuned to each other.

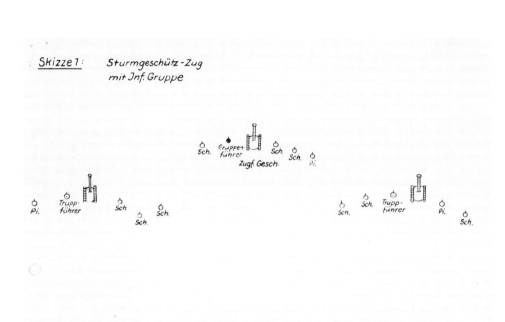

Skizze 1: Sturmgeschütz-Zug
mit Inf. Gruppe

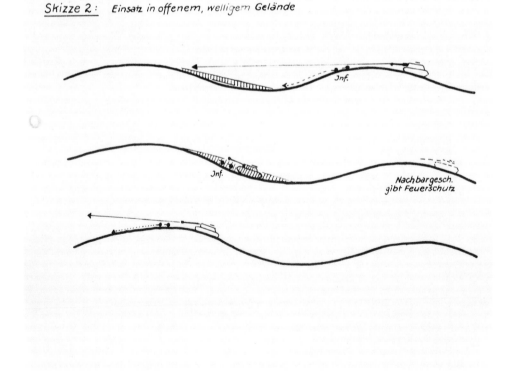

Skizze 2: Einsatz in offenem, welligem Gelände

This abandoned assault gun of StuG Brig 203 shows a hole in the cast gun mantlet. Here a machine gun with an axis parallel to the gun was installed for self-defence. This useful detail was only installed in a few assault guns.

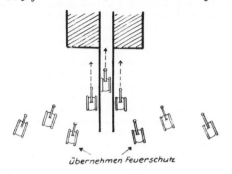

Skizze 3: Kampf gegen Ortschaften (schematisch, ohne eingezeichnete Infantrie)

übernehmen Feuerschutz

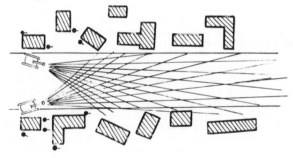

Skizze 4: Ortskampf

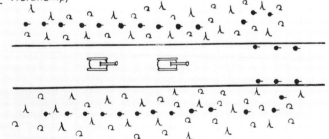

Skizze 5: Waldkampf

NOVEMBER 1944

At the beginning of 1945, the Memel front in northern East Prussia held, despite only weak German forces.

On 1 November, PzAOK 3 reported an attack by Russian aircraft in which phosphorus bombs were dropped on various villages. Parts of these villages burned down. An assault gun of the 203 Brigade also caught fire, but could be extinguished.
The eastward-defending units of PzAOK 3 tried to shield Königsberg. On 1 Nov 1944, Propagandakompanie 697 sent a success report:

> *Volksgrenadiere in the Battle for East Prussia.*
>
> *During the heavy defensive fighting in the East Prussian area between Ebenrode and Schlossberg, a company of the 561. VGrenDiv shot down nine T-34s in eight minutes... Of these nine, five were put out of action by Panzerfaust.*
>
> *The 561. VGrenDiv, supported by parts of H StuGBrig 203, destroyed over 300 enemy tanks within a week, i.e. most of the total of 442 that were destroyed by the XXVI. Army Corps...*

Under growing enemy pressure, the Organisationsabteilung (organizational department) ordered PzAbt 21 (20. PzDiv) to be sent to Grafenwöhr for conversion to Panthers on 2 Nov 1944. The high command of PzAOK 3 intervened and demanded that the tanks be delivered directly to the front.

On 5 November PzBrig 103 reported 93 SPW of which 71 were operational. Because the grenadiers were deployed purely as infantry during last few weeks, the fighting strength dropped dramatically. While there were enough drivers, the remaining soldiers were just enough to occupy the 15 SPWs. PzBrig 103 therefore reported a need for 300 trained tank grenadiers to increase its combat strength. Given the situation, this request could not be met.

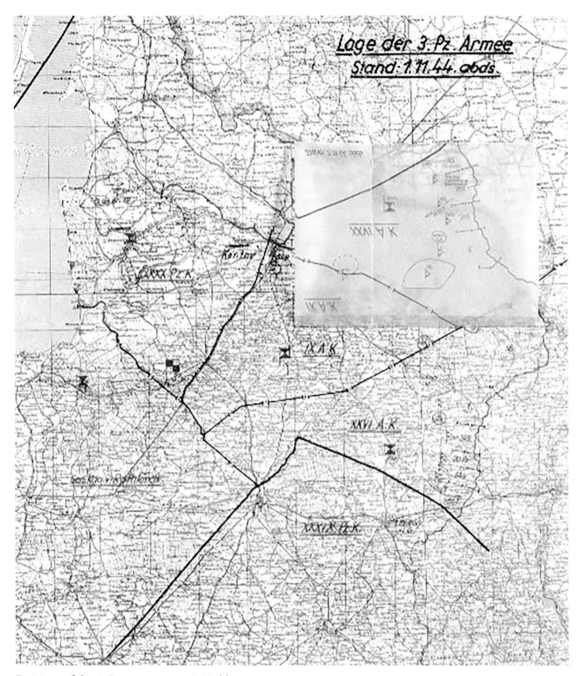

Positions of the 3. Panzerarmee on 1.11.44.

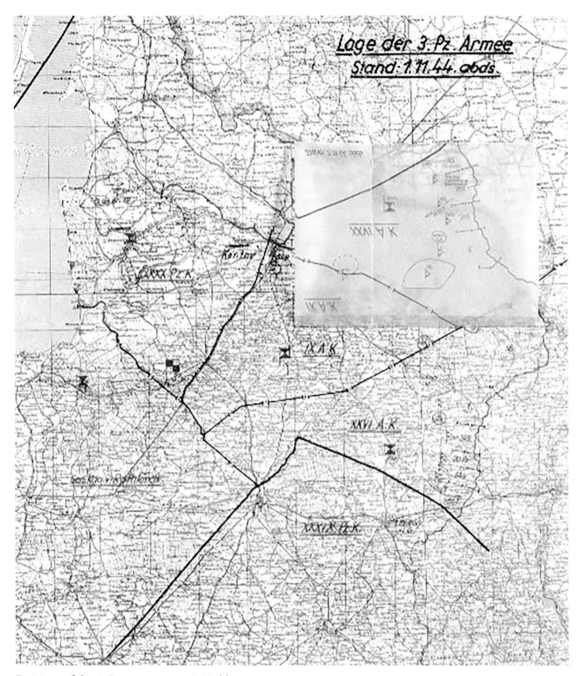
DEZEMBER 1944

On 9 December 1944, the XXVI. Armee received instructions from PzAOK 3 to establish Grenadier-Begleit companies for batteries of the existing H StuGBrig. It is however unlikely that this order could have been implemented.

JANUAR - APRIL 1945

In early 1945, H StuGBrig 203 defended east of a line from Insterburg (Chernyakhovsk) and Angerapp (Osyorsk). The River Pregel in the north and Angerapp (Angrapa) in the east formed natural obstacles. The war diary of the 3.Panzer Armee (PzAOK 3) noted at the beginning of January that the Russians only conducted attacks with limited tank support (maximum 15 - 20).

At this point, Brigade 203 was almost complete and 26 of its 31 assault guns could be reported as operational. Despite the difficult spare parts situation, the repair services were able to recover and repair defective vehicles time and again.

The men of Brigade 203 spent Christmas 1944 at Georgenburg stud farm. The war was lost – that was clear to every soldier at the time. The fight continued to protect the homeland.

On 13 January 1945, PzAOK 3 ordered H StuGBrig 203 "with 20 to 30 assault guns" to attack Alt-Preussenfelde near the Romintenstellung. In cooperation with a Festungs-PaK-Kompanie, local attacks by the Soviets could be repulsed. Due to the numerical superiority of the enemy, these successes were only of a short-term nature. In the following days, the front had to be withdrawn further and Insterburg was evacuated without a fight. Russian units continued to advance inexorably towards the coast.

On 24 January, the brigade stood in -25°C cold near Preussisch-Eylau (Bagrationowsk) not far from Königsberg (Kaliningrad). The capital of Prussia was to be almost completely destroyed a few days later by an RAF bomber attack.

In early February, Königsberg was encircled with the remnants of the 3. Panzer Armee. The last route of retreat over land had been closed by the capture of Elbing (Elblag).

At the end of the fighting in East Prussia, parts of the division were deployed as infantry. The men's equipment was barely sufficient for this and the supply of ammunition was also not assured. The spit of land called the Frische Nehrung can be seen in the background.

As the end inevitably approached, the operational readiness of 203 Brigade rapidly declined. There was a shortage of everything - food, fuel, spare parts and ammunition. The remnants of the brigade were deployed infantry-style in a helpless attempt to fend off the opponent.

At the beginning of March, the men of the "Elephant Brigade" withdrew to the Frische Haff, a natural lagoon west of Königsberg. On 20 March, orders were given to set fire to and destroy all remaining vehicles.

In view of the hopeless situation, the remaining men of Brigade 203 took the initiative. To avoid capture by the Red Army, the only route left was across the Baltic Sea. In order to reach a harbour, simple rafts were built from oil barrels and wooden planks near Balga.

The remnants of the brigade crossed to Pillau, a distance of about five kilometres. Then, north of Fischhausen (Primorsk), makeshift shelters and emplacements were built in the forest in early April. When another offensive by the Russians threatened in mid-April, the retreat to the headland of the Frisches Haff was again ordered. From Pillau, the men crossed over to the Hela peninsula north of Danzig. In the harbour town of Hela, the remnants of the brigade were embarked together with thousands of refugees and other units. The watchword was 'west', and the destination ports were often unknown. This is how many wounded arrived in Copenhagen, Denmark.

Other parts of the brigade were brought to Swinemünde (Świnoujście) in small cutters. Friedrich Gassauer wrote in his chronicle:

On 2 May we went by train to Flensburg. Before that, the death of Adolf Hitler was announced. Some of the men then broke away from the troop. In Flensburg, 20 men of the 3. Batterie were still together, including Uffz Weirich, who had been a field cook for many years. He took rations for 150 men and distributed them. Then the brigade disbanded.

The war was over.

Under the impact of the severe cold, German made uniforms were issued and the Sturmartilleristen were difficult to recognise as German soldiers.